S0-AFV-749

DATE DUE

JUL 1 2 '96		
JUL 0 1 '97		
SEP 1 7 '91		
APR 2 8 '00		

MY LOST
WILDERNESS

MY LOST WILDERNESS

Adventures of
an Alaskan Hunter and Guide

RALPH W. YOUNG

Illustrated by Bob Cary

Foreword by Bob Good

WINCHESTER PRESS

An Imprint of New Century Publishers, Inc.

ACKNOWLEDGMENTS

The story "Close Encounters" originally appeared, in slightly different form, in *Sports Afield*. I thank that magazine for permission to include the story in this book. I also wish to express my gratitude to Rich LaRocco, whose editorial advice and assistance helped immeasurably in the shaping of this book as well as my last one, *Grizzlies Don't Come Easy*.

—Ralph Young

Printing Code

11   12   13   14   15   16

Library of Congress Cataloging in Publication Data
Young, Ralph W.
  My lost wilderness.

  1. Bear hunting—Alaska. 2. Hunting—Alaska.
3. Fishing—Alaska. I. Cary, Bob. II. Title.
SK295.Y69   1983   799.29798   83-21981
ISBN 0-8329-0312-4

TO JULIA

Contents

Foreword by Bob Good   ix

Close Encounters   3
Of Bears and Men   13
The World's Most Awesome Predator   23
Never Say Die!   31
The Trophy   41
Bizarre Bear Hunts   49
The Exceptional Exception   59
The Saga of Sockless George   69

Photographic Souvenirs: A Portfolio   81

Trapping Can Be Ticklish   97
Hasselborg the Hermit   113
Fishin' Fools   125
Black Bear the Hard Way   135
When I Hire a Guide   147
Summer of the Trumpeter   157
Living with the Bears   167
Return to Alaska   181

Foreword

Ralph Young is a man who has walked among giants. For thirty years his speciality as an Alaskan guide was leading his clients in quest of North America's most dangerous big-game animal, the great Alaskan brown bear. And Ralph's favorite hunting grounds were the headwaters of the smaller salmon-spawning streams where the dense rain forests close in around you and full sunlight seldom penetrates. This is the habitat of the largest specimens of the grizzly family, and Ralph's rule of thumb was that the best trophy always lived in the thickest cover at the very head of the streams.

Here, encounters with your quarry are often measured in feet rather than yards, and a man carries his rifle in his hand, not slung on his shoulder. At these ranges, a shot, even though fired rapidly, must disable a bear in his tracks. The normal killing shot won't do. A lung- or heart-shot bear can reach his adversary in seconds and the animal's ferocity is legendary. Ralph often encountered that ferocity first-hand.

When he was living with the Aleuts, Ralph found a mangled hunter lying dead in a snow bank. The man's face had been bitten off, one arm entirely severed, and his chest crushed, as a cat would crush a small bird. A brown bear lay dead a few feet away. Although fatally wounded, his massive jaws had exacted a terrible toll in the seconds before he expired.

The physical power of an Alaskan brown bear boggles the mind. It is difficult to try to describe its capabilities in ordinary terms. Ralph tells of once finding a sea-lion carcass that weighed nearly two thousand pounds. A brown bear had carried it four hundred yards into the timber where it could be devoured in seclusion. In all my experience of hunting dangerous game on several continents, I have personally never witnessed another animal that has the stamina to absorb so many direct, potentially fatal hits from high-powered cartridges and still stay on its feet.

In the fall of 1982, I was hunting brown bear with a friend, Joe, in the Yakutak area of Southeastern Alaska. We were taking turns floating a stretch of the Situk about thirty miles outside of town. On this particular evening, it was my turn to do the pickup of the floaters at the bridge. It was getting on into evening and I was passing the time catching silver salmon as I waited for my friend and his guide. I was just landing my second fish when I heard a shot ring out about a half-mile up river. Then, in rapid succession, there was a furious volley of seven more shots, the last ending in a muffled "thump." That's the kind of shooting a brown-bear hunter dreads hearing. It could only mean a dangerous situation had developed.

Darkness fell quickly and I paced a path into the concrete bridge as I sweated out the night. In my position, I was helpless to do anything until daylight. About two in the morning, a raft bobbed out of the fog and into sight. In the dim beam of the flashlight, I could pick out both my friend and his guide. Their first words were, "We're OK." A sense of relief flooded over me.

The next day, we returned to the site of the kill. Even in full daylight, the scene was incredible. Blood, and ripped and torn brush were everywhere. Hesitantly, Joe and his guide recounted the incident of the previous evening. Just at dark, they had spotted the bear walking upstream as they were drifting down. At forty yards, Joe eased from the raft, kneeled and fired the first shot, dumping the bear at stream's edge. The nine-and-one-half foot bear was on his feet in an instant and closing. Joe and his guide fired simultaneously and the bear dropped again, spinning and rolling in the shallows only to burst up and keep coming. Eight shots in all ripped through the bear, taking out the heart, lungs, and liver, but somehow all managed to miss major bones which would have kept the bear down.

Just as they fired the last rounds in their magazines, the bear turned and plunged into the brush, running seventy long yards, ripping up brush and biting off alders before piling up dead. I have examined and autopsied several hundred big-game animals but I have never seen one that had every vital organ disintegrated in such a manner. What is equally amazing is that Joe was using a .458 magnum, a caliber I have seen drop an African elephant with a single round. Had the bear not changed his direction at the last minute, it is easy but not pleasant to imagine the result.

For Ralph Young to have guided more than thirty years for these remarkable animals under the most demanding conditions and to have never received a mauling or had a client injured, is evidence of his unique place in the history of Alaskan guides.

In Ralph's guiding career, his clients took some three hundred brown-bear trophies. Some came easy; some only after a hair-raising experience. And along the way Ralph guided the biggest names in outdoor sport. Legends like Jack O'Connor and Warren Page became both clients and friends. Barons and earls, carpenters and salesmen, they all beat a path to the door of possibly the greatest brown-bear guide of all time.

Those were the halcyon days of Alaska, and Ralph Young lived life to the fullest. He wrote this book in his late seventies, after finishing his very popular first book, *Grizzlies Don't Come Easy*. Odds are you may never venture forth after the fabled brown bear with Ralph Young as your guide; and with the winds of change that have altered the face of Alaska for all time, you'll never get to meet characters like Sockless George face-to-face, but here in the pages of this book you'll get to know them through Ralph Young. Let Ralph guide you now up the headwaters of salmon rivers and over the trails of his lost wilderness.

Bob Good
Chairman of the Board
The American Sportsman's Club

Close Encounters

During the thirty years that I was a professional big-game guide in southeastern Alaska, I saw thousands of the great coastal grizzly bears that inhabit certain of the offshore islands. These bears, commonly known as brownies, are the largest carnivores that walk the earth. They also might be the most dangerous of the world's big-game animals to hunt or to photograph.

It's not surprising that during the years I was actively guiding I had some exciting and hairy experiences. Several times I was attacked by bears that had no apparent provocation. Frequently, wounded grizzlies I trailed boiled back at me, or at least tried to. In each case I killed the attacking bear or I probably wouldn't be writing about it. I never enjoyed these encounters. However, I accepted them as part of a job I was paid very well to perform.

Many bears that ran toward me were bluffing. Others were merely coming closer for a better look at the strange, two-legged creature that had invaded their domain. These experiences were interesting, but they certainly were not hazardous. As I look back, I am convinced the nearest I have come to disaster during my career were encounters with bears that neither attacked nor even saw me. Take for example the spring I guided "Hank" Hoffman, at the time an Eastern Airlines pilot.

One afternoon we were cruising down the south arm of Kelp Bay, which is on Baranof Island across the channel from Admiralty. We were planning to hunt the big meadow at the head that evening when we spotted a medium-size but very handsome grizzly bear feeding on the beach at the base of a steep mountain to our right. Rowing with muffled oar locks, I was able to approach to within shooting range. Hank rested his rifle across the bow of the skiff and took his shot. The bear seemed to stumble, then spun around and disappeared into the brush before my friend could fire again. When we went ashore to investigate we found only a very faint blood trail that led straight up the steep mountain. It certainly was not the kind of terrain I would have chosen to trail a wounded grizzly bear. The slope was covered with a sparse growth of stunted evergreens and brush, and the angle of ascent was nearly seventy degrees. Before starting up the mountain after the wounded animal I noticed a centuries-old spruce tree standing all alone in stately majesty at about three hundred feet elevation. Obviously there had to be a bench or shelf of relatively level ground up there to support such a giant tree. I set a course for that spruce intending to use the vantage point to inspect the surrounding area where the bear might be bedded down or perhaps lying dead.

Climbing that steep slope was the toughest kind of work. Though I didn't like to do it, I had to carry my rifle slung over my shoulder to enable me to use both hands and feet for climbing. I made slow progress and lost the blood trail I had originally followed. When finally I reached my objective and just as I was pulling myself up onto the bench, I noticed the tip of a fern no more than five feet from my face move ever so slightly. Since there wasn't a breath of wind, obviously some creature had moved the plant. Suddenly I got the picture. There had to be a depression at the base of the big tree and my wounded grizzly was lying in it. It had been the bear moving its body that had caused the fern to tremble. Had I pulled myself up as I started to I would have tumbled down on top of the bear and that would have been too bad! My friend and client Hank would have had to cook his own supper that night and eat it alone.

Most carefully and slowly I eased back down the hill about fifty feet. Then I worked my way to the right before climbing to a spot where I was able to look down onto the place where I had seen the fern move. The bear was right where I suspected, in the hollow at the base of the tree. Even as I watched I saw the bear licking its left front leg where Hank's bullet had creased it. Resting my .375 H&H Magnum over a moss-covered rock, I shot the animal in the neck, killing it instantly.

After we finished skinning the bear I thought about what happened. The depression at the base of the tree, which was partly natural and partly bear made, was the beast's bed. It had been used a long while. Possibly the bear had hibernated there the previous winter. From the moment we had spotted the grizzly feeding along the beach until I had killed it, the animal had never been aware of my presence. I'll always believe seeing the fern moving saved me from disaster.

There is a time to hunt and a time not to hunt. When the wind and weather or both are unfavorable it is worse than useless to sally forth in quest of any big-game animal that I have hunted. Not all of my clients have been aware of this truism, however. Too many of them were of the opinion that the man who hunted from dawn to dark and traveled ten miles a day would surely see more bears than one who hunted only when conditions were favorable and traveled hardly at all. The fact is that most of the bears my hunters and I have taken through the years were killed when we used our eyes and brains rather than our legs.

I remember the chap who traveled more than five thousand miles from one of the states on the eastern seaboard to make a fall grizzly bear hunt with me. It was late one evening in October when we dropped anchor in a snug harbor on the south end of Admiralty Island. It started to rain before we finished eating our dinner. And it rained the next four days and nights as it can rain only in southeastern Alaska. A steady cold downpour driven by gale-force winds sent the salmon creeks flooding over their banks, forcing the bears to seek sustenance from late-maturing berries and vegetation back in the foothills.

We were warm and comfortable aboard the cruiser and there were ample supplies of food and fuel to last a month. Considering the atrocious weather I would have stayed on the boat until things improved if I was alone. It was a time to read and reflect and to rest. By my client didn't agree. He'd come to Alaska to hunt bears and by Jupiter he intended to hunt bears and to hell with the weather. So on each of those four days from dawn until dusk we slogged over endless spongy muskegs and through dreary, dripping, junglelike forests. Each night we returned to our cruiser wet, weary and discouraged. And we saw no bears.

Early on the morning of the fifth day I went on deck and was pleased to find that it had stopped raining and the wind had shifted to the northwest. The sullen cloud cover was dispersing and the snow line had dropped to about eight hundred feet. All this meant that within forty-eight hours the creek we intended to hunt would be back to normal and the bears would be returning to resume their salmon fishing. But when I told my companion the good news and suggested that we stay away from the creek another day or two and spend the time at the mouth of the bay shooting at seals, he went into a tizzy. Did I think he had traveled all the way across the continent and halfway to the north pole to shoot at seals? No! He had come to Alaska to hunt grizzly bears and that's what he intended to do. The smart professional guide doesn't argue too much with a paying client. So that morning, against my better judgment, we started hiking up the still-flooded creek.

From the start it was the meanest kind of traveling. Though the creek was falling, it was still too deep to wade except in a few places. Consequently, we had to fight our way through a nearly impenetrable jungle of brush that bordered the stream. Our progress was so slow that at noon I estimated we were upstream barely two miles. In all that long dreary morning we had seen no fresh bear sign. Convinced there wasn't a grizzly bear on the watershed, we made no effort to travel quietly going downstream. We carried our rifles slung over our shoulders instead of in our hands where they belonged. We really weren't hunting. Our main objective was to get out of that miserable jungle as quickly as possible.

The light was beginning to fade late that afternoon when we came to a huge spruce that had blown down during the storm. It was about four feet in diameter and spanned the creek from bank to bank. Beyond the windfall I could see an opening in the timber where the woods ended and the tidal flat began. In a few minutes we would be out of the awful jungle and into open country. The fallen tree had an immense root structure nearly twelve feet high. It somewhat resembled a lattice fence. Between these roots and the eroded bank was a clear passage six feet wide. Before entering this corridor I should have taken a look over the log to see what might be on the other side. However, instead of taking this elementary precaution I walked in behind the roots that were vertical to the stream bed. I was nearly through when for some reason I stopped and looked back. My hunter was standing in midstream seemingly petrified. His jaw was slack and he was pointing at something across the log with his extended right arm. I hurried back alongside my companion. In the lee of the big spruce windfall were three grizzly bears—a sow with two yearling cubs. Had I taken another step or two I would have walked right into their midst! Almost certainly I would have been severely mauled or even killed. Even worse, I might have been crippled for life.

I picked up a couple of baseball-size rocks and clicked them together. It's a sound that bears hate and fear. Huffing and snorting, they bounded up onto the bank and disappeared into the cover. Later, as we passed going downstream we heard the female growling back in the heavy timber that bordered the creek. That evening I thanked the Good Lord for telling me to stop and look back before taking that final step.

The professional hunter of dangerous game is not permitted to make many mistakes. Sometimes he is not permitted to make even one. Eternal vigilance is the price he pays for his life and livelihood. When he forgets or becomes careless, his career may end painfully and abruptly. Here's an example of what I mean.

I was guiding the late Wilbur Littleton of San Antonio, Texas. Wilbur, who was one of the finest hunters I ever knew and a complete gentleman, made five expeditions with me over a period of years. This, his final trip, was strictly to photograph bears in their natural habitat and at as close range as practical. Bears were plentiful that summer, and early in the trip we gathered enough good footage of bears, bears, and more bears to edit into an outstanding sixty-minute documentary movie. We decided to use the remainder of our time trying to secure color moving pictures of salmon in the process of spawning. So we moved operations over to a large stream at the north end of Admiralty Island where giant king salmon were spawning.

Getting close-up, detailed footage of salmon spawning requires proper technique, good weather, and lots of patience. One day while Wilbur was waiting for a pair of salmon to start performing it occurred to me that there really was nothing I could do at the time to help my friend. I told him I would take a hike up the river to a side stream I knew swarmed with pan-size trout and catch a mess for supper. Now, the prime consideration of a guide is the safety of his client. Consequently, although the chance that he would be attacked by a grizzly during my absence was extremely remote, I left my bear rifle with my friend just in case the unthinkable did occur. Then, carrying only my flyrod and a pocket knife, I set off upstream.

Thirty minutes later I came to the small tributary creek where there was a pool full of trout. I was making my way toward the head of this pool, skirting the brush, when I nearly bumped into a grizzly bear cub that couldn't have weighed more than forty pounds. I knew I was in trouble when the little fellow squealed as a pig does when its tail is twisted. That cub's mother had to be very close by. I dropped my custom-made flyrod into the water and dove headlong into the brush. Seconds later the female came tearing out of the cover at the head of the pool uttering a series of chilling, coughing roars. She sniffed her cub briefly, gave it a sharp slap with her paw and then raised her head at a forty-five degree angle, testing the air. Perhaps she picked up a trace of man scent. In any case she went into a terrible rage and I'll never forget what followed . . . a demonstration of raw, unbridled, insane savagery. She raced through the pool like a runaway locomotive. Once she stopped for a moment and let loose with a fearsome roar that could have been heard by any creature within two miles. My mouth was powder dry, the skin over my forehead was taut, and my heart was beating so rapidly I thought it would burst. There was a knotty hemlock sapling about five inches in diameter and tough as hickory growing near the border of the pool. It would have taken no small effort to chop it in half with a trapping hatchet. The bear tore it up by the roots and nearly severed it with one snap of those mighty jaws.

I really can't say how long the enraged brownie continued to demonstrate, but when she finally quieted down and left the scene with her still frightened cub at her heels, I was greatly relieved. Shortly afterward I heard the cub squeal back in the woods a hundred yards or so. Ten minutes later it squealed again far up the valley a quarter of a mile distant. I retrieved my flyrod from the pool where I had dropped it. In the now quiet pool I could see great numbers of trout lying near the bottom but I had no stomach for fishing. Nor did I feel heroic, as I went down the river, the skin still tight on my forehead and my heart stuttering like an outboard motor warming up on a cold morning. When I returned to Wilbur he looked at me curiously. "No trout?" he asked.

"No trout," I answered.

That evening as I was cooking supper and while my friend was labeling the film taken that day, he remarked, "I heard a brownie roar up the river today while you were gone."

"So did I," I said.

And that's all either of us ever mentioned about the incident.

Another close encounter drives home the point that grizzly bear behavior is unpredictable and that the traveler in bear country must always expect the unexpected.

It happened one summer while I was out on Admiralty Island living with the bears and trying to learn what I could of their behavior and habits. One beautiful August day I went up a stream about half a mile above tide water. The salmon were just starting to run in the creek, and few bears were in evidence. In fact I hadn't seen one that day. It was such a warm pleasant day (a rarity in southeastern Alaska) that I decided to take a nap. I stripped off my heavy woolen shirt and cotton undershirt and spread them out on the gravel as a bed. Bare to the waist, I stretched out, face up to the sun, and promptly fell asleep.

Some while later I opened my eyes and found myself looking into the face of a grizzly not more than three feet from my own. Probably the bear had been prowling the stream looking for salmon when it had spotted a strange creature lying on the gravel and had come over to investigate. At the moment I opened my eyes I believe the bear was about to sniff me! My reaction was purely instinctive. I scrambled for my rifle lying alongside, and I think I yelled. The reaction of the grizzly was equally instinctive. It bolted for the heavy cover bordering the creek without a trace of dignity.

Men often act strangely under duress. In this instance I put on my two shirts, smoothed out the wrinkles, washed my hands and face in the stream, and combed my hair with my fingers. Then, although there wasn't another person within thirty miles, I said in a voice that would have carried well in Madison Square

Garden, "In the future I'm going to be more careful where I take a nap." If the red gods were watching that day, I'll bet they chuckled a long while afterward.

Of Bears and Men

Many years ago when there were more bears in Alaska than people, I was sitting on the bank of an Admiralty Island salmon stream with a client watching for a grizzly bear to show itself. It was a peaceful scene for an Admiralty salmon stream in September. Salmon splashed in the creek, ravens talked in the adjacent woods, and a bald eagle perched in a nearby snag, waiting patiently for a salmon to die so that it might pick the flesh from its bones. Suddenly a sow grizzly followed by a lone cub came out of the brush below us, walked across the creek and disappeared into the woods on the opposite side. That's all that happened. Two bears walked across the creek. Later that same day as we were discussing it, my companion mentioned the *three* bears we had seen crossing the stream.

"Two bears," I corrected him.

"Three bears," he insisted.

"Two bears."

"Three bears!"

"All right, dammit, three bears!" I said.

Even at that stage of my career I had learned not to argue with a paying customer.

There is a vast army of individuals who simply cannot be factual when it comes to bears. Most of these people are reasonably honest in other matters. If they catch a twelve-inch trout, it's a twelve-inch trout; let them shoot a four-point buck, it's a four-point buck. But if they kill a three hundred pound bear, it weighs half a ton.

A certain doctor I once guided was a charming gentleman and a model of integrity. However, one day he casually mentioned killing a six hundred pound black bear in Arizona, a year or two previously. I didn't dispute his statement, but I asked him what he did with the bear.

"Took it to town," he said.

"How did you get it in?" I asked.

"Oh, just threw it over the saddle horse."

Now, that was some bear. Some horse, too!

Just the other day I received a report concerning an Alabama man who claimed to have killed a bear in that state recently that weighed eight hundred pounds. The wet hide purportedly measured *thirteen* feet from nose to tail. Imagine that! Why, an adult giraffe stands only seventeen feet tall. The hunter claimed this horrendous bear was in full charge when killed. I don't believe that either.

The estimated poundage of a bear is usually much greater than its true weight. I have weighed a few trophy-size male black bears that were killed in the spring. Their average weight was about two hundred and fifty pounds. Of course, the bears would have been as much as forty percent heavier if taken in the fall season. During my career I have seen thousands of black bears, and I have skinned a few hundred. I have never encountered a blackie I thought would weigh much more than five hundred pounds, and very few that were that hefty.

The great coastal fish-eating grizzlies of Alaska, the so-called Alaskan brown bears, are the largest land carnivores that roam the earth. It is seldom that one of these beasts has been actually weighed in the field. One that was, however, weighed slightly more than thirteen hundred pounds. This bear was killed on Kodiak Island early in the fall. Nobody claimed it was the largest bear ever killed. Also, it might well have weighed more had it been taken later in the season. I have a hunch that out on the Alaska Peninsula, or Kodiak Island, or perhaps in the Yakutat region may live an old buster of a brownie that might weigh fifteen hundred pounds. It's hard to visualize such a bear—a bear larger than a trophy-size Yukon moose; three times the size of a male Bengal tiger; half again the weight of a saddle horse! Perhaps some readers will be disappointed to learn that these bears aren't as large as they are frequently reported to be. As I see it, they are large enough. If they were any bigger, I'm not sure I would have made a career of hunting them.

Another misconception concerns the widely believed tale about bears throwing salmon from a stream. One respected authority described in considerable detail how Alaskan brownies strike salmon from the water. The man never saw an Alaskan bear unless he saw it in a zoo. Nor did he, or anyone else, ever witness one of these bears strike a salmon from the water with its paw. That's not the way bears fish. Bears pounce on the fish and carry them ashore in their mouths. I'll pay $100 a foot for motion picture film showing bears striking fish from a stream. I'm not interested in still photos because they can be faked. I first made this offer thirty years ago in a popular magazine and I have never had a response.

When self-styled bear authorities get off on the subject of the ferocity of bears, even blackies, the truth really takes it on the chin. When looking over my collection of back issues of outdoor literature, I find one author who said he was treed by a black bear. Maybe, but since most blackies climb trees much better and faster than men, there's not much point shinnying up a tree to escape one. You might as well jump into the water to escape a hungry shark! Another armchair philosopher writes that just being in the same area with a grizzly bear is enough to provoke an attack. Later in the same tale this chap relates that bears sometimes turn hunters themselves and trail a man who thinks he is pursuing the bear. Most intriguing of all is the writer who credits bears with understanding and practicing the rather difficult military tactic of ambush.

When I was guiding bear hunters, I used to wish those writers would soft-pedal that stuff. They were scaring some of my clients before we even went afield. Getting a person in such a state of mind to within reasonable shooting range of a grizzly was not easy. One client of mine panicked and ran when we just happened to come onto an unsuspecting grizzly that was feeding on a patch of sedge. The bear panicked and ran also—in the opposite direction. One moment there were three of us in a relatively small area. A few seconds later I was all alone. It was downright silly.

But the worst case was a woman I guided many years ago when I knew less about bears and people than I do now.

This lady had been brought to Alaska by her husband for the specific purpose of shooting a grizzly bear. In anticipation of the hunt this female had read every book she could find on the subject of bears. She had found gore dripping from each page. The result was that by the time we reached the hunting areas she was seeing bears in such unlikely places as under the table aboard our cruiser. The first few days we hunted, her husband accompanied us as an observer. However, when he discovered that bear hunting interfered with his drinking, he decided to stay aboard the boat and play solitaire with Jim Beam and Old Granddad. Out alone with me and without the moral support of her husband, the woman refused to enter the woods. Too dangerous. Might get ambushed, you know. She was going to kill her bears out in the wide open spaces or not at all. One day we spotted a fair-size bear on the opposite shore of a tidal flat we were watching. It was about a mile away and barely visible to the naked eye. By taking advantage of gullies, sloughs and patches of tall grass, we had a good chance of stalking the beast within reasonable shooting range. We had covered only half the distance when she put on the brakes. It was as close to the grizzly as she cared to go. I reasoned with her. I told her the bear wasn't aware of our presence. I assured her there was absolutely no danger. She wasn't convinced. Finally I took her by the arm and gently but firmly coaxed her closer to the bruin which was still a long quarter mile away. At last she dug both heels into the sod and refused to budge another inch. "We're close enough, we're close enough," she kept muttering.

"Close enough for *what*?" I asked her. "Why, that bear's so far away it would take the post office three days to deliver a postcard to it. Come on, let's get within rifle range at least."

It was nothing doing. The little lady was just as close to that bear as she intended to go. I reasoned, I pleaded, I threatened. I used every trick of the guiding trade I knew to no avail. With mule-headed obstinacy she stood pat on her inalienable right to travel or not to travel any place she wished. Finally I gave up.

"All right, then," I told her, "we ain't gonna get that bear."

She pouted. "If you were as good a guide as they said you were, you'd find *some* way to get me that bear."

I did, too. Leaving the lady huntress safe behind a drift log in the middle of the tidal flat, I stalked and killed the grizzly. My female client was happy, I was happy, the woman's husband who thought his wife had killed the bear was happy, everybody was happy. Except maybe the bear.

It's hard for the average hunter to be realistic and objective about bear behavior. It isn't easy to see things from the bears' viewpoint. These animals spend about half of their lives in hibernation. As a result, a bear when not sleeping is eating or seeking food to sustain life and to build up a reserve of fat to live through the cold months when no food is available. There is no time to play or frolic or gallivant about looking for trouble. Otters and deer and wolves play and engage in mock battle seemingly in sheer exuberance and from an excess of energy. Bears never do. To the bruins, life is a serious business. Except for the brief time spent breeding, they live to eat. They have no time or inclination to seek trouble. Bears are solitary creatures. They avoid each other. I have often seen two male grizzlies pass each other within a few feet on a salmon creek, each utterly ignoring the other. If a bear, any bear, encounters a man, it will usually retreat. If it gets the man's scent it will not only retreat, it may panic. During the years I traveled extensively in grizzly habitat, I would meet up with bears that probably had never seen a man before. Unless these bears had picked up my scent, some of them would come closer for a better look. I've even had bears run toward me. Perhaps they were trying to scare me away or bluff me. When I didn't bluff or retreat, the bear invariably left the scene after a certain amount of huffing and blowing to impress me and to maintain its dignity. You have nothing to fear when meeting a bear in a wilderness area, providing you maintain sense and poise. If there is any trouble—if there is an attack—it's almost invariably the man who causes it.

I do not consider black bears dangerous. I am speaking of wild black bears, of course. During those years when I was a professional bear hunter and guide, I encountered thousands of blackies under every possible circumstance. I have never seen a black bear show fight. Oh, I know there are exceptions. People have been attacked by black bears. I suppose any animal will attack if sufficiently frightened or harassed. I have a scar on my left hand where I was bitten by a squirrel I picked up when I was a kid. Another time I went close to a moose that had just given birth to a calf. The old girl resented my action and chased me into the river. Still, I don't consider squirrels or moose dangerous animals. For all that, we continue to read and hear tales of red-eyed, foam-flecked, slavering, roaring black bears attacking hapless citizens strolling through the woods. I don't believe these stories.

Numerous sportsmen who have hunted big game in Africa, India, southeast Asia and elsewhere, have told me that they consider the Alaska brown bear the most dangerous animal in the world to hunt or to photograph. I don't see how any animal could be more dangerous than one of these great golden-coated monarchs when encountered in the jungle that borders every salmon creek in southeastern Alaska, if the beast has been unduly harassed or wounded. No writer of fiction ever painted in words a true picture of an enraged grizzly bear making a determined, life-or-death attack. There aren't many men who have faced such an attack, and some of these didn't survive to relate the experience.

Many years ago when I lived on Afognak Island, which is just across the channel from Kodiak, two natives went hunting Kodiak bears. They each carried Winchester Model 94 .30-30 rifles. These weapons are adequate for hunting deer in brushy country but certainly not proper for shooting the huge bears of that region. In the course of the hunt, the men wounded a bear which escaped into the heavy alder growth that covered the hillside. One of the natives started to follow the Kodiak. His partner, who was less brave or smarter, stayed below. A while later, the smart native heard a single shot. When his companion didn't return, he went back to the village and reported the incident.

The following day four of us formed a party and went back to investigate. We found the native lying on a snow field partway up the mountain adjacent to a thick patch of alders. His rifle with an empty shell in the chamber was lying alongside him. And he was dead. He had been roughly handled by the bear. His jaw was crushed, and one arm and a leg were broken. Most impressive were the tusk marks on the man's chest. The bear must have picked him up and shaken him as a dog does a rabbit. Later I found the bear a short distance away where it had crawled and died. Although I have tried to be objective concerning bear behavior, since that day up on the lonely mountain on Afognak Island, I have never taken the Alaskan coastal grizzly bears lightly. The profound respect I had for these bears during the years I earned my living guiding hunters is one of the secrets of my longevity.

Why do so many people fabricate tales about bears doing impossible things? Although it's true that occasionally a bear will die hard—take terrible punishment before expiring—the same is true of a mouse, a deer or a man. That doesn't alter the fact that bears and men are basically the same physically. Each has lungs, a heart, and a brain. A bear with any of these vital organs ruptured by a high-velocity bullet of proper construction will die, and quickly, too. Still, weird tales continue to be heard of bears traveling fantastic distances with heart and lungs shot out. One writer of a tale published in a now defunct magazine told of a wounded grizzly that kept charging after a section of its backbone had been blown out. I wonder if some of these people who tell such tales really believe such nonsense themselves.

Once while I was attending a social gathering, the host took it upon himself to entertain me by exhibiting his collection of photographs. One of these was a photo of a rather diminutive dead grizzly lying in the time-honored pose with the hunter's rifle propped against its side.

"Know what that is?" my host asked.

"Looks like a dead bear," I said.

"Sure it's a dead bear, but what kind?"

"You tell me," I said. "I don't know much about bears."

He smiled condescendingly. "That's a grizzly bear."

"Gosh. Kill him yourself?"

"Yep. Killed him while he was charging me."

He pointed his finger at a spot between and just above the bear's eyes. "See that white spot?" he asked. I said I did.

Know what that is? That's where a .30-06 bullet splattered on its head. Took two more bullets in the heart to stop the bear."

I left the party shortly after. Outrageous liars weary me.

This notion of the thickness of a bear's skull is well established but has no basis in fact. Actually the skull of the largest of these animals is not particularly massive. The bone at the forehead may be an eighth of an inch thick and will not deflect any high-speed big-game bullet, regardless of the angle at which it strikes. An eagle can pick through a large bear's head with its

20

beak. The ordinary .22 Rimfire bullet easily penetrates a bear's skull and goes into the brain. Grizzly bears have been killed with rifles of this caliber.

I'm ready to believe practically anything I read or hear regarding the strength and agility of grizzly bears. The power contained in half a ton of bear bone and muscle can hardly be exaggerated. This is particularly true of the fish-eating coastal grizzlies of Alaska. Here, fact meets fiction at last. These huge bears have been known to drag the carcass of a bull moose up a steep mountainside through thick alder growth. They pack a deer as easily as a cat does a mouse.

The most awe-inspiring display of pure brute force I ever saw occurred on Afognak Island many years ago when I was a young man. A native and I had found a grizzly bear trap and decided to catch a Kodiak with it. One evening we set the trap in a bear trail and fastened it to a cottonwood tree two feet in diameter with a heavy boom chain. When we returned the following day we had a fair-sized bear caught by the right front paw. The native with me was afraid to leave the skiff and go ashore to kill the bear. I was just as scared as my companion, but I had a conscience. Someone had to kill that bear, so I took the native's .30-30, which had a broken magazine spring, and went ashore alone. Since the weapon was capable of firing only a single shot without reloading, I had to get up close to the beast to get in a fatal shot to the brain or spine. As I slowly advanced, the mighty animal reared up and struck the tree such a blow with the forty-pound trap that it shook the limbs far above. It had broken every one of its tusks biting the cruel trap and snapping at the tree. In another few hours, the bear might have had the cottonwood down. I actually feared he would break the trap chain and get to me before I could kill him. Finally I got a shot into the brain and ended the encounter.

After we skinned the bear and took as much meat as we could to give to the people in the village, I took the trap and dropped it overboard in a deep part of the lake. One experience like that was enough.

The World's
Most Awesome Predator

The Alaska brown bear is a specialized form of the grizzly that inhabits interior Alaska, western Canada and a few wilderness areas of Montana, Idaho, Washington, and Wyoming. The range of these mighty carnivora is Alaska's southern coastland, which stretches in a great semicircle from the British Columbia border west and north to the tip of the Alaska peninsula, plus certain offshore islands, including Kodiak, Baranof, and Admiralty.

It's a lonely land these wilderness monarchs inhabit. Here a man might wander for days, weeks, even months and see no other living soul. It's a beautiful land of towering peaks, dark forests, glaciers that are older than history, blue lakes, mighty rivers, brawling salmon streams, valleys clothed in willows and alders, gray seas and still estuaries. It's a bountiful land where each summer and fall millions of salmon come out of the Pacific and enter hundreds of unnamed streams to spawn. There are many lush meadows where the grass grows taller than a man and a dozen varieties of wild berries flourish. It's a quiet land where only the call of eagles, the songs of migratory birds, the music of running water and the moaning of the wind break the silence.

Any estimate of the brown bear population in this vast

primitive region is at best a calculated guess. I cannot believe there are fewer than five thousand bears here, and there may be twice that many. The greatest concentration of these bears is probably on Admiralty Island in southeastern Alaska. During the Golden Age of bear hunting in Alaska in the 1950s and early 1960s I estimated that there was nearly one bear to the square mile on this wonderful island, which is now a designated wilderness. Alaska game officials say the brown bear population is relatively stable with an increase in numbers in a few areas and a decrease in others. Be that as it may, there certainly are not as many trophy-size bears as there were thirty years ago. It takes ten or twelve years for a brown bear to reach maximum size, and with the present and increasing hunting pressure not many bears live that long.

During my bear hunting career, I guided clients from all parts of the United States as well as several European and South American countries. These hunters took about three hundred trophy bears. For each bear killed I'm sure we passed up twenty others we didn't want or couldn't stalk. In addition to the experience I gained guiding hunters and photographers all those years, I often went out alone in the summer and lived with the bears. Carrying only my rifle, sleeping bag, and an absolute minimum of equipment, I ate the same food as the bears, walked the same ancient trails, and sometimes appropriated their dens and beds for shelter and rest. I even tried to think like a bear, but I doubt that I succeeded. Several times I slipped up onto sleeping bears and observed their behavior. They toss and turn and even snore while slumbering just as a man does. On these expeditions I won't say the bears accepted me as one of their own, but they did tolerate me. During the hundreds of days I lived on intimate terms with the bears on Admiralty Island, I never fired a shot at a bear.

Through the years I learned a lot about bears, and the more knowledgeable I became the greater was my admiration and respect for these monarchs of the wilderness. However, I don't consider them dangerous in the manner of man-eating tigers or rogue elephants. Bears don't stalk and devour human beings, nor do they go rampaging through villages, destroying lives and property. Bears are by nature solitary creatures that tend to avoid contact with man. But when bears are unduly harassed, threatened or wounded, their ferocity and ability to inflict frightful damage to a human can hardly be overstated. I have never taken Alaska brown bears lightly. Some of my clients have, however, and in a couple of instances their attitude might have had tragic results.

The late Warren Page, noted gun writer and hunter, made five Alaskan bear hunts with me. The first trip was just too easy. Though the hunt was scheduled to last twenty days, he killed his limit of two brown bears in a single day, and the action was hardly more exhilarating than shoveling snow or digging for clams at high tide. When Page returned for a fall hunt a few years later I found that he had a low opinion of Alaska brown bears as dangerous game. Compared to African lions and Cape buffalo, brown bears were pussycats, he said.

One day early in the trip we were wading up a small brushy creek on Baranof Island. There were plenty of salmon and the bears were obviously feeding on them. The place practically shrieked of bear. I was expecting to see one every moment.

As we moved upstream, the creek became narrower and the brush thicker. Late in the afternoon with twilight approaching we moved around a bend in the stream and came face to face with a brown bear that was traveling down the same waterway that we were ascending. The bear was trophy size and not more than forty feet distant. It was a touchy situation. Anything might happen.

"Shoot that bear!" I said.

But Page wasn't ready. By the time he got his rifle unslung and managed to get off a hastily aimed shot, the beast had almost reached the bordering berry brush and devil thorn. The bullet creased the animal's rump, inflicting a superficial wound.

Instantly the big bear gave a savage snarl, reversed its flight, and charged us. At the same moment a blow primer from one of Page's handloads jammed the action of his rifle. For a fraction of a second the man who was destined to become one of the world's most famous big-game hunters stood with an inoperable rifle facing a life-or-death attack by an Alaska brown bear. The bear was within twenty feet of us when I stopped it with a .375 bullet into its chest.

Never again was Page contemptuous of brown bears. He'd been lucky. Had he been alone that day, he would have learned too late how extremely dangerous these bears can be.

The late Jack O'Connor was probably the most well-known big-game hunter of the century. Jack made two brown bear hunts with me—the first in the spring of 1956 and the second a few years later. On the first trip Jack killed two bears, one of which was an outstanding trophy taken under difficult conditions. On the second hunt, Jack made it clear that top priority should be given to getting his wife Eleanor a good representative brown bear.

"I don't really care if I fire a shot the entire hunt," Jack said. "I want Eleanor to shoot a bear like I got last time around, and I would like to watch her do it."

I took the O'Connors to a little-known remote tidal meadow on the east coast of Chicagof Island. It was one of my favorite places to hunt bears but because of the difficulty of access I seldom brought clients there. The meadow was about a mile long and half that wide. Near the head was a wooded island with an elevation of some fifty feet. I decided that Eleanor and I would take a stand on this island where we could watch the upper part of the meadow, leaving Jack at the lower end where he could keep that area under observation. Before separating I mentioned to O'Connor that I wished he had brought along his rifle that day.

"What for?" Jack said gruffly. "Eleanor's doing the hunting

today. When she gets her bear, then I'll start hunting. Until then I don't need a rifle."

"I still wish you were carrying your rifle," I answered. Then I told my friend that if we spotted a bear worth stalking from our position on the island that I would signal for him to come up. Perhaps he would enjoy watching the action and maybe get some photographs of his wife stalking and shooting an Alaska brown bear. Jack thought that was a fine idea. I also suggested that since he wasn't carrying a rifle he should remain where he was unless I signaled for him to move up. O'Connor agreed that was proper procedure.

As the shadows lengthened and the long sub-arctic twilight approached, two small bears came out of the forest and began grazing on the tender lush sedge near our position. Once I saw Jack signaling vigorously and pointing toward his left. Swinging my binoculars in that direction, I spotted a fair-size bear near the edge of the woods. The animal had a badly rubbed rump so I gave Jack the no-no signal. Finally the sun disappeared behind the mountains and a chill was in the air, but there was still plenty of light left when a magnificent trophy-size brown bear with an unblemished pelt strode out of the spruce forest and, exhibiting supreme arrogance, walked into a depression and began feeding. Judging by the bear's actions, I guessed that the brute would remain in the same area for an hour or more, browsing on the tender sedge that grew there. So, leaving Mrs. O'Connor to keep the big bear under observation, I went back to signal Jack that we had a bear in sight and to come up and join us. I watched until Jack left his position and started walking up a dry waterway toward me. Then, to my dismay and horror, I saw a female bear followed by two small cubs enter the stream bed and begin walking rapidly *down* the waterway toward my unsuspecting client. The bears and O'Connor were on a collision course. My mouth went dry as I watched the wilderness drama unfold. Neither the man nor the bears were aware of each other's presence, but in a few minutes there would be a confrontation and anything might happen. Sows with cubs are extremely volatile and prone to attack if they think their offspring are threatened. I had to do something, but as I considered the options it seemed that anything I did was fraught with disaster. Then suddenly the female stood erect on her hind legs, raised her great head to a forty-five degree angle and tested the air. She must have picked up a trace of the dreaded man scent because just as suddenly she dropped to all four feet and streaked toward the woods followed by both cubs. When Jack caught up with me he was totally unaware how nearly he had come to walking into a nasty situation.

Hunting brown bears with rifle or camera can be exciting even when nothing out of the ordinary occurs. It's exciting to be wading up a salmon creek and hear a raven talking to a bear back in the thick stuff. Ravens eat fish but they can't catch them. So when a bear catches a salmon and carries it back into the woods to devour it, a raven eager to scavenge the scraps will often perch in a tree and scold the bear. Several times my clients and I have taken trophy bears that we located by listening to the ravens talk. To be traveling along a bear trail worn deep into the ground by the countless thousands of bears that have walked it for centuries and suddenly smell a bear you cannot see is sure to start the blood pumping. If it sounds improbable that you might smell a bear before seeing it, let me assure you it has happened to me several times while roaming in the junglelike forests of southeastern Alaska. Hunting Alaska brown bears may at times be enervating, wearisome or disappointing, but to me it's high adventure and never boring.

Brown bears grow larger on Kodiak Island than anywhere else in Alaska. Also this island has been the locale of so many early hunting expeditions that the terms brown bear and Kodiak bear have become synonymous in the minds of many people. Actually a Kodiak bear is simply a brown bear that lives on Kodiak Island. All Kodiak bears are brown bears, but not all brown bears are Kodiak bears.

The World's Most Awesome Predator

The best time to hunt Alaska brown bears is in the spring. This is true whether the sportsman hunts on Kodiak Island or in some other part of their range where they may be more numerous. When these animals come out of hibernation in April or May, depending on the local climate and severity of the winter, their pelts are prime, dark and luxuriant. The sooner a bear is taken after emerging from its den the better because in a matter of a couple of weeks or even a few days the pelts become rubbed. By June most of the hides are worthless. Spring bear hunting is not arduous. Mainly it's a matter of patiently scanning the slopes and tidal meadows with binoculars until a suitable trophy is spotted. Stalking a brown bear is not difficult either, if you can correctly gauge the wind currents. It's impossible to stalk a bear downwind. Their eyesight is notoriously poor. Strangely enough, a brown bear will spook at the sound of a breaking twig or a scuffing of gravel but will often ignore ordinary human conversation. I have met bears far back in the interior of Admiralty Island that were not in the least alarmed when I shouted at them, but they fled when I picked up a dry limb and broke it over my knee!

Fall bear hunting requires considerably more physical effort compared to spring hunting, but I consider it more interesting. Certainly it's more hazardous. In my career I have faced seven or eight determined and unprovoked attacks by brown bears. I do not believe it's a coincidence that all of these occurred while I was guiding hunters in southeastern Alaska on brushy, constricted salmon creeks in September and October. Patience is the secret of spring bear hunting, but in the fall it's persistence that pays dividends. You don't wait for the bear; you go after him. I like hunting brown bears in the fall on the salmon creeks. I like the challenge; I like the element of danger; I like to think this type of hunting is truly fair chase with the odds sometimes favoring the hunted. As I said, the critters are unpredictable.

Never Say Die!

As an Alaskan big game guide, I was fortunate to hunt with many of the most famous sportsmen in North America. I was also acquainted with some highly skilled hunters who had never received much attention or acclaim. One of these was a lad who was strictly a meat hunter and who lived in an obscure Indian village in southeastern Alaska. He killed at least three hundred deer before he was old enough to shave. He was the one who taught me to call deer using a leaf held between the teeth. Another was an old-timer I knew for forty years. I don't remember him ever going deer hunting without coming back with a buck. I must add that sometimes he didn't return for three or even four days. And then there was Allen Hasselborg who lived alone on Admiralty Island for fifty years. As a young man around the turn of the century he had hunted the great coastal grizzly bears on that island for their hides. Later he became a famous guide. He may have been the greatest bear hunter of modern times.

I would say that most of the truly great hunters I have known were excellent to superb riflemen; others were mediocre. Some were fine physical specimens; others were not. A few had

31

excellent eyesight; just as many wore glasses. I hunted with men who glided through the woods as silently as timber wolves; others made as much racket as a horse heading for the barn. One man who may have been the most famous big-game hunter since World War II was downright clumsy!

But rich or poor, famous or unknown, mighty or humble, each of the eminently successful hunters had one thing in common— a quality compounded of patience, perseverance and a never-say-die stick-to-itiveness. Many of my clients would not have taken the trophies they did had we not hunted hard right up to the last hour and even the last minute of an expedition.

I once booked a client from Switzerland for a ten-day hunt early in May. I never cared for these abbreviated trips but my client's business schedule didn't permit a longer one at the time. To make matters worse, he arrived a day later than scheduled. This allowed us only eight full days to hunt. Considering that the limit was three blackies and one brown or grizzly bear at the time, we had our work cut out.

We started hunting black bears on the mainland about forty miles south of Juneau. The bears were just starting to come out of hibernation and weren't as plentiful as they would be later. It took us six days to take our limit of blackies.

Even before we anchored up in a safe cove on Admiralty Island in grizzly country, it began raining and blowing hard from the southeast. That evening when we left our cruiser to hunt the sedge flats at the head of the bay we were lashed by a cold, penetrating rain driven by gale-force winds. Bears don't enjoy foul weather any more than do bear hunters, so it's not strange that we saw only one bear during the entire long dreary evening. It wasn't much of a grizzly. It was small, scrawny and badly rubbed. It was a sorry representative of the grandest and most formidable animal on the continent. I pointed the beast out to my friend.

"You didn't travel halfway around the world to shoot a creature like that, did you?" I said.

"No," said my client, "I did not!"

It was dark when we returned to our boat wet, cold, and hardly brimming with enthusiasm.

The weather on the final day was even worse than on the preceding one. We stayed aboard the boat most of the day listening to the wind moaning in the rigging and watching the tall spruces bend and sway in the gale wind. In the outer bay we could see the whitecaps rolling ominously and watched the spume blow into the woods like snow. With five hours of daylight remaining, we left our cruiser dressed in foul-weather gear. Risking disaster every foot of the way, we made our way through the stormy seas in my fourteen-foot skiff to a partly sheltered cove that was bordered on the windward side by tall spruces. I placed my client in a position where he could see the entire upper part of the cove. I moved around a wooded point where I could watch the rest of the area. The time passed slowly. Except for an occasional deer that came out of the forest to feed, and a few gulls that flew around, uttering plaintive calls, there was no evidence of wildlife. At intervals I would slip around the point to see how my client was reacting. Each time I could see him right where I had left him eagerly scanning the cove with his binoculars. I felt sorry for him and damned the weather that was fouling up his chance of getting his coveted trophy. If ever a man deserved to get a good grizzly, my Swiss friend did.

We had no more than thirty minutes of shooting light left when suddenly my sport came sprinting toward me. "A big dark brute!" he shouted. I picked up my rifle and binoculars and followed him. Just as we came out of the woods I saw the broad rump of an enormous grizzly move into the dark forest on the opposite shore moving downwind. These big Alaskan bears travel at a steady four-mile-an-hour gait when on the prowl. Down the shoreline about half a mile was a tiny sheltered cove. The bear would be there in a few minutes. Our only chance to intercept the bear was to reach the cove before the bear. It was impossible to row the skiff laden with equipment and a passenger in the stormy seas fast enough to get downwind of the traveling bear. But we couldn't just stand there and watch our trophy escape us. We had to try! First I cut the shoreline to save time. Then throwing caution to the wind I cranked the motor and drove the boat before the wind to the point of recklessness. I swung wide of the cove and came into it with the wind in our face. As I beached the skiff my hunter scanned the fringe of timber upwind. It was nearly too dark to distinguish objects.

As I was securing the boat I heard him say, "I see something."

"Do you see the bear?" I shouted.

"I see something," he repeated. "I see something big and dark. It's moving!"

"Shoot!" I said.

At that moment I saw what my client was looking at through his rifle scope. At the crack of the rifle the object disappeared.

Leaving my companion to watch the skiff I took my rifle and flashlight and ran toward the woods to investigate. I found the bear lying dead just inside the heavy timber. The bullet had been perfectly placed and the beast had moved only a few steps before dying. I rolled it over onto its back for skinning the next morning and returned to my friend.

"You got yourself a bear," I said.

"He's not as big as I thought he was, is he?" he asked.

"No," I said. "He's bigger!"

So our persistent refusal to accept what appeared to be impossible odds got us a splendid trophy. And we did it literally in the last minute of the final day. My friend returned to his homeland happy and in a mood to recommend me to his friends in the hunting fraternity.

Unfortunately not all of my clients reacted favorably to the adversities and disappointments that can come with hunting bears in Alaska. One chap I remember well arrived for a September trip with vigor and enthusiasm oozing from his pores. He begrudged the time spent going through the necessary procedure of acquiring license and bear tags. He fidgeted when I checked over his outfit to make certain he had all necessary and proper clothing for Alaska weather. During the seven hours it required to reach bear country in my cruiser he wore himself out pacing the deck, sorting and fiddling with his equipment and chain-smoking cigarettes. By the time we arrived where I intended to start the hunt, he was too tired to go ashore even to sight in his rifle.

We had no trouble picking up a suitable black bear the first day, but when we moved over to Admiralty Island for grizzlies things went less smoothly. Although there was a fair number of salmon spawning in the streams and we saw numerous sows, cubs and immature males we couldn't locate a trophy-size bear. It was an old story to me. Many times in my career I have faced a similar situation. I knew that if we continued to hunt hard and move about from one creek to another that we would surely find our trophy. But my companion's original enthusiasm rapidly disappeared. As one unsuccessful day followed another, his face took on the mournful expression of an unemployed bloodhound. It depressed me just to look at him.

When finally the last day of the trip arrived with no grizzly hide salted down in the barrel, I decided to spend the day on Mole River, which had a good concentration of bears and where we had taken many fine trophies through the years. We hunted as far upstream as there were salmon. We saw well-traveled trails along both banks, fresh sign and numerous partly devoured fish but nary a bear. It was obvious that my client had given up entirely. He dragged along behind me, he showed no interest, he wasn't looking for bears, and the aura of his defeatism was so strong I could almost smell it. Late that evening we came to a bend in the stream where bear sign was particularly plentiful. Aloud I said, "Where in hell are all the bears?"

My companion looked at me sadly. "There aren't any bears!" he croaked. The guy had given up. He was beaten.

Down the creek a bit farther we came to a salmon that had

35

been bitten by a bear and carried onto a gravel bar. It was still bleeding and alive. The wet tracks of a grizzly led from the fish into the woods. I looked up on the low sidehill and saw the bear that made those tracks standing broadside looking at us. My client was staring blankly at his feet. I grabbed his arm and shook him roughly.

"There's your bear", I said. "Look where I'm pointing. Wake up, dammit. Shoot that bear!"

Had my hunter been alert and hunting instead of moping, he would have got his trophy. As it happened the bear disappeared into the brush before he was able to get into position to shoot. I had a strong urge to tell him he didn't deserve to get a bear. However, I remained silent, and I'm glad I did.

Fifteen minutes later we came to the mouth of the river. About two hundred yards away our skiff was bobbing in the rising tide. I saw something else too. Beyond the skiff and traveling toward us was a bear, and on the opposite shore farther away but within stalking distance was another. As I was sizing up the situation a third bear larger than either of the others came striding down a small tributary creek less than one hundred yards distant. My hunter didn't see any of these animals because as far as he was concerned the hunt was over. Once again I shook his arm and pointed toward the nearest bear. He made a good shot and killed the bear, which is about the only thing he did right that day.

So, two hundred yards and a few minutes from the end of our hunt my client got his coveted Alaskan brown bear trophy. But it wasn't due to any degree of perseverance, nor an attitude of "never-say-die" on the part of this chap who traveled to Alaska from a faraway land to hunt the great bears!

Once and only once I nearly tried too hard. I pursued a course of action contrary to my client's explicit desire and took a dangerous gamble. It might well have resulted in having my guide license revoked and my career terminated.

It happened back when the seasons were long, the limits

generous, and the bears plentiful. At the time I had an enviable reputation as a guide. I had never taken a client on a hunt without getting at least one bear. In my correspondence with prospective clients, I practically guaranteed bear trophies. In fact, in some cases I made the promise, no "bears, no pay!" It was a foolish thing to do. I was treading on very thin ice.

One of these hunters to whom I had promised more than I should have booked the last fifteen days of the spring season.

We got two black bears with no difficulty, but when we moved to Admiralty Island for the big browns, things went less smoothly. Though we hunted in some of my favorite places and saw a fair number of bears, we didn't encounter any trophy-size animals with prime pelts. Time was beginning to become a factor, so I decided to move operations to a large bay on the west coast of Baranof Island, where spring comes much later than on the other islands. The first evening we cruised up a long, narrow, steep-walled fiord where the snow lay deep on the beaches until we came to a broad tidal meadow where I had hunted many times. A game trail that had been used by countless generations of bears skirted the bordering timber and extended the width of the meadow. Sixty feet from this bear highway was an ancient drift log. Here we took our stand. Any bear that traveled the trail would pass us broadside, offering a shot that even a novice could scarcely flub. All we had to do was wait and watch. It was up to the bears now—to the bears and the gods of chance.

I scanned the snow fields that towered above the meadow with my binoculars. I could plainly see two fresh bear trails in the deep, powered snow. The big brownies were starting to come out of hibernation. Each day more bears would be showing. Very soon one or two or more of them would come down from the snow fields and walk the trail we were watching. We had only to be patient and wait.

No bear showed that first day though we stayed on our stand as long as there was sufficient light to see through our sights. I wasn't too disappointed and certainly not discouraged. We had three more days to hunt—plenty of time for my client to get the bears I had promised he would. I remember saying to him that evening, "You'll get your bears!"

We spent the next two days at our stand facing the bear trail and didn't leave until there was no shooting light left. Although I could distinguish fresh new trails in the snow fields, not one bear showed anywhere on the broad meadow. Our spirits drooped when a cold, chilling rain began to fall on the evening of the third day.

That evening at our cruiser it was obvious that my hunter was becoming anxious. He wanted to know why I insisted on hunting the same spot every day in spite of seeing no bears or even bear sign. Wouldn't it be better, he asked, if we returned to Admiralty Island where we had seen all those bears a few days previously? What difference that so many Admiralty grizzlies had rubbed pelts? After all, a less than perfect trophy was better than no trophy at all. I could only reply to this argument that we were in the right place at the right time. The bears would surely come. We had to have patience. The trip wasn't over yet.

On the final day of our scheduled fifteen-day hunt we returned to the stand where we had been the three preceding days. Before the sun went down behind the mountains it was almost balmy. The sedge and beach rye were definitely greener and taller. Spring was about to burst upon us like a pent-up flood. It was bear weather. Today we would see bears. I was sure of it. But we didn't. In all that broad meadow with its luscious beds of sweet sedge and other succulent vegetation not one bear came from the snow fields to feed. We were a despondent pair as we sloshed toward our skiff in the near darkness that evening. Aboard our cruiser my client ate sparingly and went to bed without speaking a word.

I lay in my sleeping bag a long while that night thinking of the trip that had begun so fortuitously and ended so dismally. If only we had more time, even another day. There was the answer. I'd extend the trip a day or two, or as many as it took to get my client the bears I had promised. With this decision made I fell asleep and didn't awake until late the next morning.

When I informed my sport that we would hunt another day the stuff hit the fan. Absolutely no, he said. He had signed a contract with me for a hunt between two specified dates and if I didn't honor that contract, he would take legal action when we did return to civilization, whenever that might be. Though there was no doubt in my mind that he meant what he said, I replied that we would hunt another day and that was that!

That evening about 8 o'clock we were back at our stand facing the bear trail when a magnificent brownie with a perfect pelt came out of the woods half a mile upwind and started walking the trail in our direction. When he was broadside to us my hunter clobbered him. Before I had finished skinning the animal another bear even larger than the first came out of the woods and traveled the trail toward us. My client killed it also. Two splendid trophies in less than an hour!

From that moment until I saw my client off at the airport in town all was sweetness and light. With his arm around my shoulder he told me I was undoubtedly the greatest guide in Alaska if not the whole world.

But to this day I shudder to think what might have happened if those two bears hadn't come down that trail that evening so many years ago.

The Trophy

When Alaska was a true frontier I hunted deer for sustenance or profit—never for sport. Because earning a livelihood by more conventional means was difficult and abhorrent to my nature and instincts, and because I had a family to provide for, I was a market hunter on a modest scale. I sold deer at bargain rates to whoever would buy them, including some of the better families in town.

Being a meat hunter, I shot only fat does without fawns or immature bucks. I passed up any deer that I thought would weigh in excess of one hundred and twenty-five pounds. But once I shot what I am certain was the largest buck deer I ever saw in the forty-two years I lived and hunted in Alaska. I did it deliberately—not for the meat but for the trophy value. I lived to regret it.

At the time I lived with my family at the edge of the town of Petersburg on Mitkof Island. Two hundred feet from our door began an unpeopled wilderness of virgin forest, muskegs, meadows, ponds and mountains that extended for six hundred square miles. In the interior of the island a man could wander an entire season and never see another living soul. The area teemed with wildlife. It was the breeding ground of ducks, geese, even trumpeter swans. It was inhabited by hundreds of black bears, furbearers, and great numbers of grouse and ptarmigan. Thousands of Sitka blacktail deer made this wilderness wonderland their home. Things have changed since then; but in those days it was a little bit of paradise in a ravished and despoiled world.

One morning in September of 1941 I told my wife, "We'll have fresh liver for supper."

"Can I depend on that?" she asked.

"You can," I answered.

Carrying only my Model 99 Savage .300 caliber lever-action rifle, a few cartridges, matches and a piece of half-inch Manila rope, I started across the vast muskeg, which extended a mile to the base of the mountains in the background. Two hours later I was in the high country.

The winter of 1940–41 was one of the mildest on record. As a result, the winter deer kill had been minimal and the deer population was near the saturation point. I could easily have killed a deer or two that day at a lower elevation but I was young and strong and healthy and loved to be up in the mountain meadows. It always seemed to me that the sky was bluer, the water sweeter, and the wild blueberries more delectable in the Alaska mountains than anywhere else I've been. It was good to look over onto the mainland with its mighty peaks and glaciers, the home of bears, moose, and mountain goats. In the far distance I could see Admiralty Island where there probably was a grizzly bear for each of the island's sixteen hundred square miles.

For a long while I sat basking in the warm autumn sun, enjoying the grand scenery and listening to the voices of the wilderness. Then I plucked a leaf, placed it between my teeth and sucking in air in a manner taught me by an Indian, I gave the call of a fawn in distress. Within the next several minutes I called up no less than seven deer. All were does except one buck that came sneaking along behind the others, the way bucks do when they hear a fawn call. I could easily have shot any one of those deer but didn't. I was sure I could get a deer at a lower elevation closer to town and save the labor of packing the meat off that mountain. Those deer walked up there of their own volition, and I had no intention of carrying them back down.

At the time, a local store was offering a spanking new Model 94 .30-30 Winchester to the person who shot the biggest deer in the area that season. To qualify, the recipient had to be a resident licensed hunter who presented a legally taken deer, field-dressed, whole and in good condition.

The shadows were lengthening, the air was getting nippy, and I had feasted on enough blueberries and I had seen enough deer that I didn't want to shoot for one day. I decided it was time to start for the low country and toward home. I hadn't gone far when I came to a very likely looking place to see game. More out of curiosity than anything else, I blew my call once more. Almost immediately a fat doe came bounding toward me as though she had springs attached to her hooves. Her eyes were large as saucers and the ears pointed straight over her muzzle like two blunt horns. She looked almost hysterical as she searched for the fawn she had heard, all the while snorting as deer do when excited. I called once more to tease her and watch the reaction. I was watching the antics of the doe when suddenly a huge buck walked out of the cover where I had first seen the doe. And such a buck!

Alaska deer (Sitka) do not average as large as the blacktails farther south in British Columbia, Washington, and Oregon. Only rarely do Sitkas qualify for the Boone and Crockett record book in the blacktail category, but this one would have made the list with points to spare.

He walked in the trail of the doe, placing his feet daintily and proudly like the king of the high country. The buck must have weighed in excess of two hundred pounds and had a body

43

shaped like a barrel. His swollen neck was like that of a stallion, and he carried a perfectly matched set of antlers—five points on each side. Suddenly I wanted that deer. And not for its meat. I wanted that neck and head and rack mounted and hanging on my wall at home. I wanted a trophy! I raised my rifle, aimed at the base of the neck, squeezed the trigger and watched the deer drop without a sound or a quiver.

After I dressed out my prize, removed the liver and carried the entrails into the brush for the scavengers, I fashioned a harness from a piece of rope and attached it to the animal's neck. Then I stripped down to my underwear, trousers and boots. I made a pile of these excess clothes, placed my rifle on top, and started dragging my deer. Though the terrain sloped downhill, the ground was soft and spongy, making dragging the big deer exhausting work. When I had moved my burden about one hundred yards, I shucked off the harness and while resting went back to retrieve my clothing and rifle. In this manner I relayed the deer and my possessions a short mile until I came to the brink of a cliff. Beneath was a steep slide covered with a dense growth of alders and brush.

I dragged my deer to the edge of the slide and shoved it over. The big animal rolled and bounced down the steep incline, flushing out a covey of ptarmigan. The carcass had nearly reached bottom when a black bear came tearing out of the cover below it. The beast raced across a small clearing and rapidly disappeared into the timber. I wish some of those people who tell us that blackies are slow, cumbersome creatures could have seen that bear travel. I don't know how fast it was running but I'm sure no greyhound could have caught it!

Had I known at the time as much about the habits and behavior of black bears as I did later in my career, I would have shot that bear . . . or tried to.

From the base of the slide where my deer lay, a dense rain forest extended about one mile to the open muskeg. Once I reached the muskeg, dragging the animal the remaining distance to town was, in a manner of speaking, a piece of cake. But getting it through the junglelike forest with its ravines, windfalls, ridges, patches of devil thorns and swamps, entailed labor of heroic proportion.

I had covered barely a quarter of the distance through the jungle when the light began to fade. I laid my big buck over a log, belly down, and started for home in high gear. I hadn't traveled more than a few hundred yards when I came onto a fine forkhorn buck standing motionless, starting at me. I shot it in the neck. Fifteen minutes later I had the deer dressed out and hung in a hemlock tree to drain. Then I traveled at my best possible speed to get clear of those woods before total darkness set in.

That night when I laid a deer liver in the kitchen sink my wife remarked, "So you got one."

"I got two," I said.

"Well, in that case, it looks like I have a canning job to do."

When I left home the next morning, I was traveling light. I didn't even carry my rifle. With two deer to relay home I certainly didn't intend to pack any unnecessary equipment.

It was good daylight when I came to the place where I had hung the small buck. The deer was gone! I found bear hair on the bark of the tree. Close by in the soft ground were fresh bear tracks and a well-defined trail where the beast had dragged the carcass. Without my rifle there was no point following those drag marks into the jungle. So I moved to where I had left my trophy buck. When I reached the top of a low ridge and looked down into the swale where I had laid it over a log, I could see it wasn't where I'd left it. Then I spotted it lying close by in a patch of brush, and draped over the body was what, at first glance, appeared to be an enormous black bear, sound asleep.

When I went down for a closer inspection, I could see that the bear was only average-size. It appeared much larger because of being bloated with the huge quantities of meat it had consumed. When I yelled and shouted, hoping to frighten it away, it only

45

stared at me stupidly, like a drunk far gone in his cups. I pelted the critter with whatever I could find to throw, but the bear refused to budge. Finally I calmed down and faced the fact that the bear was in full possession of my deer and there was nothing I could do about it. So I retraced my journey back through the rain forest and across the muskeg to town, talking to myself all the way.

The following day, the third one of this fiasco, I made the long trip back, once more, to where I had left the bear draped over my prize buck. This time I carried my rifle in case the beast wanted to contest property rights with me. I also had a canvas sack to carry whatever meat I could salvage. But when I looked over the ridge into the depression below, all was quiet and peaceful. No bear was there and very little deer either. Another bear, or two, or God knows how many, must have joined in the feast because there wasn't much left of that animal. What the bears hadn't eaten they had mutilated. I managed to bone out fifteen pounds or so of meat from the Sitka that must have weighed one hundred and eighty pounds field dressed. Along with my small sack of meat I took the skull and rack and started the sad journey home. I reflected with grim satisfaction that at least I had the antlers for a trophy to show for three days of labor and frustration.

I hid the skull and rack in a patch of woods near town to season. Late that fall, before the winter snows began, I went back to retrieve what was left of the hard-won trophy. The skull was gone. It simply wasn't there. Someone wandering about in the brush must have picked it up. It's probably hanging on *his* wall. To this day I have no trophy to hang on the wall of my home—not even a stuffed squirrel. No mounted trophy to show for more than half a century of big-game hunting. I doubt that I ever will possess a trophy. I'm a meat hunter!

Bizarre Bear Hunts

Before the despoilers came to build roads and to clear cut the valleys, there was on Admiralty Island a cove that must have been one of the loveliest spots on earth. It was a favorite feeding ground for big Alaskan brown bears. They visited the cove in the spring to graze on the lush, sweet sedge that grew at the edge of the tidal zone and in the fall and late summer to catch the salmon that ascended the river to spawn in wondrous numbers. I took some of my favored hunters there. In those days not many other Alaskans visited the cove, and those who did respected nature, for I never saw a tin can, empty bottle, or even an ax mark to mar its pristine beauty. I shall always remember the unspoiled cove with fond nostalgia, and I shall remember also two bizarre events that occurred there during my bear-hunting career.

The first happened in the spring of 1950 when I guided a client from Lubbock, Texas. He was one of my favorite hunters. Not only was he a true sportsman and fine companion, but he never complained about the weather, the food, the accommodations or of any of the things that are incident on a wilderness big-game hunt. But he was firmly convinced that he was an

49

unlucky hunter. When he stepped off the plane that brought him to Alaska he told me, "I'm the unluckiest hunter you'll ever meet."

The hunt started auspiciously. On the very first day at the head of a long arm on Kuiu Island we took two representative black bears. In fact, three hours after we had started stalking the first blackie, I had finished skinning out the second bear. With two fine, prime pelts lashed to my packboard and headed back to our snug cruiser, I said to my client that it looked as though he had left his bad luck back in Texas. "Trip's not over yet," was my friend's laconic answer.

The following day we moved over to Baranof Island to hunt the big coastal grizzlies, more generally known as brownies, that live there. We hadn't hunted long before I began to take seriously my client's obsession about being an unlucky hunter. We saw bears every day we hunted and a fair percentage of them were suitable trophies, but somehow we couldn't connect. Each time we made a stalk something would happen. Sometimes the wind would shift and the bear would pick up our scent or the grizzly would start traveling in the opposite direction. Twice, just as my client was getting into a position to shoot, a bear moved into dense cover for no apparent reason. Finally with time running out and, no grizzly pelt salted down in the keg, I decided to move over to my secret cove on Admiralty Island.

It was a beautiful, sunny evening with several hours of daylight left when we drifted into the cove with the rising tide and took up a position at the head where we could see the entire area. The wind was favorable, visibility perfect, and the weather almost balmy. Blue grouse calling from the surrounding hills and the gabble of resident Canada geese and mallards made sweet music. Thirty or forty Sitka blacktails, lean, patchy survivors of the previous winter, browsed along the fringe of the timber. A family of playful otters, all shiny and glistening, came down the creek. When they saw us, they came closer to investigate, all the while chirping like birds. Then they left us and went frolicking down the stream and into the bay.

We had been on our stand about an hour when the first bear of the evening appeared. It was a quarter mile away but even at that distance and without using binoculars we could see that its pelt was badly rubbed. Later a sow with two cubs that couldn't have weighed more than thirty pounds each came out of the woods quite close to us. I didn't care to have these visitors so near in case we had to make a stalk in their direction, so I stood in plain view and clapped my hands loudly. All three of the bears scrambled back into the woods. Another average-size bear or two showed that evening, and then the long sub-arctic twilight began—that magic period when a really large brownie is most apt to appear.

An hour of good shooting light was left when a truly magnificent brownie appeared about a thousand yards away. The bear came out of the woods and strode majestically to a patch of sedge and began feeding. We were in a perfect position to stalk the animal. All we had to do was move a bit to our left until we were in the lee of a rocky ledge that stuck out from the timber and walk right up to the bear in perfect concealment. Twenty minutes later we reached the ledge. I sneaked a look around the corner and there was our bear seventy-five feet away, quartering toward the woods and unaware of our presence. I motioned to my hunter to step out and take his shot. At the crack of the rifle, the huge bear spun around and lunged for the woods. I went right in after him. I found the animal standing in a small opening in the deep gloom of the rain forest as though in a state of shock. I really believe the beast would have dropped dead in a matter of a second, but to be sure I placed a 270-grain soft-nose bullet from my .375 Magnum at the base of the neck, and it was all over.

Moments later my client came up, and when he saw his bear he was as happy as though he had struck oil. He was positively ecstatic! He stroked the great beast and ran his hands through the rich, heavy fur. He examined the huge head, the teeth and the awesome paws. All the while he kept up a steady, crooning monologue.

"Isn't he a beauty?" he kept saying. "Have you ever seen a more beautiful bear? How much does he weigh? I never thought I'd get a bear like this. Hell, I never thought I'd get *any* bear."

Then he finally settled down and became more practical. What was the chance, he wanted to know, of letting the bear lie out overnight so that we could return the next morning with camera to take pictures. I said we could leave the bear overnight, there was always a chance that another bear might come along and disturb our trophy. Such a thing has happened. "But," I said emphatically, "I'll take care of that possibility."

Now it happens that at the time I was wearing a heavy woolen jacket that I had bought in Canada. It was made of virgin Australian wool, and I've never had another jacket comparable to it. Worn over double-layered underwear and a woolen shirt or sweater, it had kept me warm in every type of weather that southeastern Alaska could produce, and that's saying a great deal. In all the years I had owned this jacket, it had never been laundered nor, perish the thought, dry cleaned. As a result it had acquired a distinctive odor compounded of outboard motor fuel, campfire smoke, bear grease and plain man scent. I was sure that the faintest smell of this bit of clothing would spook any bear that came near it. So before we returned to our snug cruiser that evening for a hot dinner and a bear hunter's dreamless sleep, I draped my jacket over the back of our trophy grizzly.

When we returned the following morning the sun was shining brightly and the birds were singing, but as we entered the woods the scene that met our eyes was enough to make the angels weep. During our absence a bear or a family of bears had come onto our beautiful trophy and utterly ruined the pelt. From the shoulders to the lower part of the body it was ripped and torn beyond repair. As much as forty pounds of the meat had been devoured along with parts of the hide itself. Undoubtedly the culprits responsible for the damage were bedded down nearby sleeping off their binge, and I was tempted to hunt them down and have my revenge. However, I decided not to do that—it wasn't the bears' fault we had lost a prime trophy; it was mine.

After I had finished salvaging what I could from our bear, I looked about for my jacket. It was nowhere in sight. So I started searching for it in the nearby brush where it might have been dragged. I couldn't find it. Then, while my client packed the pitiful remnant of our trophy down to our skiff, I carefully combed the cover within a radius of a hundred feet. I found no trace of my jacket. Later that same spring I returned to the cove and spent the better part of a day systematically searching the area within a quarter mile of where our bear had lain. I looked everywhere, under fallen logs, under the roots of big trees, in ravines and even into the overhanging limbs of spruce and hemlocks. I never found my jacket and to this day I do not know what happened to it. I felt sure a bear would never go near it. Maybe the old coat didn't smell that bad to them after all.

I used to know an old Indian who lived in the village of Kake on Kuprenof Island. I came upon this venerable Indian one winter while I was trapping in the area and did him a small favor which he never forgot. Years later he told me that a witch might have taken my jacket. But more likely, he said, it was the work of the mischievous spirits who live on Admiralty Island, the same ones who trip the feet of travelers so foolish as to walk in those somber forests at night.

Another strange event occurred several years after the coat incident while I was guiding a businessman from New York State. The client made three trips with me and I developed a fondness for the old gentleman. He possessed nobility of character rarely found in men these days, however he was not an easy man to guide on a wilderness bear hunt. He suffered certain physical impairments due to an automobile accident years before that severely limited his mobility, and his eyesight was not the greatest. He also used a rifle on his first trip that I wouldn't have considered suitable for hunting jackrabbits, much less one of the world's most dangerous big-game animals. It had an oversize muzzle brake fitted over the end of a twenty-five inch barrel that threw the weapon out of balance; the scope was improperly aligned and was fitted too close to the shooter's eye; the seal had been broken on the sight so that the lens was usually hopelessly fogged, and the stock appeared to have been constructed by a Neanderthal with a stone ax. The whole weapon must have weighed nearly thirteen pounds.

Early on this first hunt my client managed to shoot a fair black bear that was so close to us that I could have hit it in the eye with a spruce cone. But when we moved over onto Admiralty for brownies, each day became an exercise in frustration. On this trip we saw many bears and the sport shot in the general direction of several of them. However, except for a small grizzly that he shot at point-blank range when it reared up on its hind legs in front of us out of tall grass, my friend never drew blood. At the time the limit was two brownies or grizzlies to the license, so with time getting short I decided to take my hunter over to my favorite cover and see what happened there.

On the evening we came into the cove it was raining hard and a cruel wind howled down the valley from the snow fields above. In a very short while our hands and feet were numb from the cold and we were so chilled that had a bear come out of the woods within rifle range we couldn't have fired a shot. Something had to be done. I considered building a fire but decided against it. There was too much chance of the smoke swirling about and ruining any chance of our seeing a bear that evening. I told my hunter we would take a brisk walk toward the other side of the meadow and return to get our blood circulating and to shake off the chill. When we reached the opposite shore we were pretty well thawed out. As we turned around to retrace our steps I saw a large brownie come out of the woods close to our original position and walk down into a gulley where I knew the sedge grew particularly thick.

As we sloshed back through the mud flat, I wanted to move fast, and the old gentleman did his best, but to me it seemed a long while before we came close to the gulley where the big bear had disappeared. Then, suddenly I saw the bear's back as the huge beast started to come up out of the depression directly toward us. Instantly I squatted down in the mud and pulled my friend down alongside me. "Get ready to shoot." I said. If the bear continued to travel on its present course it would be on top of us in a matter of seconds. I slipped the safety off my big magnum. It was getting close; now it was almost too close. Wondering why the client hadn't shot, I took a quick glance at him. The man had laid his rifle down and was wiping the lens of his spectacles with a wet handkerchief! At that moment, the bear saw us for the first time. It stood up on its hind legs for a better look. Then, expelling its breath with a loud *whoosh*, the grizzly ran back into the gully with surprising speed and moments later disappeared into the woods, its broad rump looking as wide as the back of a ten-ton truck. My companion finished wiping his glasses, fitted them over his nose and calmly asked, "Now, where's that bear?" For one of the few times in my career, I was speechless. I had had all I could take for one day, and we returned to our cruiser. However, before leaving the cove I stepped off the distance from where we had squatted down in the mud to where the great bear had stood glaring at us. It was eight paces.

Rain fell hard all that night, and the wind in the tall spruces sounded to me like a dirge.

The next day the weather had taken a turn for the better. I knew that the rain of the previous night had washed away any lingering man scent we might have left, so decided to hunt the cove one more day. We had scarcely settled on our stand at the head of the flat when I spotted a fair-size grizzly feeding along the edge of a long slough that drained into the cove about one mile away. Without wasting time trying to point out the feeding bear to my companion, I started the long stalk, with my client following close behind me. It was a long, time-consuming stalk, but I never took my eyes from the bear. We skirted along the edge of the forest, took advantage of depressions in the ground, sought cover whenever possible and finally when I came to a windfall no more than fifty feet from the unsuspecting bear, I turned to tell my hunter to step forward, rest his rifle over the log and take his shot. But my friend wasn't there. He was gone! I took a quick look around and there he was on the other side of the slough, stalking some object that I didn't immediately see.

It happened that many years before an unusual combination of an extremely high tide and gale-force winds had brought a drift log into this slough and deposited it at the head of the slough. Seen from a distance it looked uncommonly like a very large bear lying in the grass. My client was stalking the log. Meanwhile the grizzly we had started to stalk had spotted the action across the slough and, not liking what he saw, had gone back into the woods. I could hear it moving about in the brush behind me. There was nothing that I could do, so I sat with my back against a small cedar and made myself comfortable.

My client was doing a beautiful job of stalking—I couldn't have done better myself. He slithered along through the mud, using his elbows for propulsion, occasionally raising his head carefully to peer ahead, then dropping down again to resume his slow forward progress. I felt sorry for the old gentleman who had traveled thousands of miles and spent a substantial sum of money to stalk a log in Alaska. At last he reached a grassy hummock where he slid his rifle onto an elevated spot and aimed carefully in the direction of the drift log. Then he released his rifle, picked up his binoculars and stared ahead a long while. Finally, holding his rifle as a man does a shotgun when moving across a field where he expects a pheasant to flush, he slowly advanced toward the piece of drift. By the time I caught up with him he was gazing down at the log sadly. Turning toward me with a sheepish expression he said, "You'll never know how utterly foolish I feel." But he was wrong. I know exactly how he felt. He felt just as I did when I stalked that very same drift log back in the spring of 1942!

The Exceptional Exception

By and large, the bear hunters I guided must have been the finest people that lived on this earth. I suppose that every one of them hoped to get an outstanding, bragging-size trophy, one that would make the record books or win an award. A surprising number of them did. One of my clients, in fact, killed the largest bear of its species ever documented as being taken in Alaska at that time. Most of my hunters took representative trophies that any experienced hunter would be happy to possess. Some of my hunters had to settle for bears that I rated as second class and that I was not proud of. However, regardless of the size or quality of the trophies taken over a period of three decades, most of my clients were unduly appreciative of my efforts to make their hunts successful and pleasant. These wonderful people, many of whom became lifelong friends, accepted the hardships, disappointments, misfortunes and outrageous weather as mere incidentals to the glorious adventure of hunting bears in Alaska. There really cannot be very much wrong with the human race as long as there are people like those with whom I hunted bears long ago in Alaska, when the nights were shorter, the skies bluer and the meadows greener than they seem to be now.

But there were exceptions. There are always exceptions. The standout, the exception above all others, the exceptional exception, was a chap I once guided from Texas whom I will always remember and *never* forget.

Before contracting to take this gentleman on a spring bear hunt, we exchanged references, as was usual. I was vastly impressed by the information he offered. He wrote that he had hunted lions, rhinos, Cape buffalo, and heaven knows what else in Africa with a redoubtable white hunter. Later, so he claimed, he had made an expedition into the Central American jungles for jaguar. More recently he had hunted Kodiak bears with a noted guide. I was flattered to think that this man who had hunted big game with the elite of the outfitter-guide fraternity now desired to hunt grizzly bears with me.

When he arrived in Alaska, I was disappointed by his appearance and deportment. He didn't look, talk, or behave like any experienced big-game hunter I had known. He seemed to be unduly concerned about trivial matters. One of his first remarks was that he hoped I had engaged a competent cook because he suffered from a nervous stomach. After I assured him that our cook specialized in preparing meals for hunters with nervous stomachs, as well as for those with flat feet, tired hearts, and tennis elbow, he wanted to know if I would guarantee we would arrive back in town exactly on schedule. He said that it was very important that we did arrive back as planned because he had a date with his wife to meet her at a specified day and hour at Disneyland. If he failed to keep this appointment, his wife was sure to be extremely unhappy, and when his wife became unhappy she was meaner than a wet tomcat with its tail tied in a knot. I assured the man that we would return on schedule barring some unforeseen misadventure. Finally, it disturbed me when he carelessly tossed his rifle, which he carried in a cheap, flimsy case, into the back of my station wagon with the rest of his baggage. I like to see a client with whom I am going to hunt grizzly bears treat his rifles with loving care and respect.

Early in the trip I discovered this man from Texas had not been favorably impressed with his former guides. One, he said had a short temper and drank whiskey. He complained another was more concerned with the safety and well-being of his dogs than of his clients. After listening to this fellow's poor opinion of these guides, I decided that he wouldn't think well of my performance, either, regardless of how the trip turned out.

One evening early in the hunt we spotted a fine, prime grizzly feeding at the edge of a tidal meadow, close to a patch of heavy cover. It was not an easy stalk, but we managed to get within reasonable shooting range, and I told my client to take his shot. It took him an uncommonly long while to maneuver into an awkward shooting position and to get off a shot. I saw the sod erupt two feet ahead of the unsuspecting bear, which swapped ends and disappeared into the brush in something less than one second!

Right away my man began making alibis. The range was too far. His scope had fogged. His finger had slipped on the trigger at the crucial moment. The ammunition was defective. While he was thinking up more excuses I shot, offhand, at a rock near where the bear had been feeding. I hit it nearly dead center. I ought not to have done this because it must have embarrassed my client. However, I have to tell this tale the way it happened.

Early one afternoon later in the trip, we left our floating camp with the skiff and headed for the tidal meadows at the terminus of a long inlet about fifteen miles away. It was an area greatly favored by the grizzly bears. Here they came to feed on the rich growth of sedge, and one of the best-traveled bear trails on all of Admiralty Island skirted the shores of this unspoiled, beautiful wilderness wonderland. At first everything seemed to be propitious. The wind and tide were favorable and the weather reasonably good for May in southeastern Alaska. We settled

61

down near a point where we had miles of prime bear country under observation.

Deer began to appear at the edge of the woods all along the shoreline as the tide receded and evening approached. Later, an occasional small grizzly came out of the woods to feed on the new growth of sedge. These bears were fun to watch, but we had no interest in them as trophies. What I wanted and hoped to see, was a big male on the prowl for a mate. I urged my client to be alert and vigilant and stressed how important it was that we see any big boar grizzly before it became aware of our presence. When I finished my pep talk, my hunter said that he was hungry and asked whether I had anything to eat. I gave him an apple, which he then squirreled away in a pocket of his hunting coat.

There were still two hours of good daylight left when a brisk breeze began blowing up the channel. At first I thought it was no more than a spring squall. However, an hour later, when it began raining and blowing harder, I decided that we had best call it a day and start for camp. By the time I had maneuvered our skiff down the creek into deep water where I could safely use the motor, the wind had increased to near gale force. Bucking into the whitecaps we soon became drenched with saltwater spray and our skiff soon began shipping water. Then when one cylinder shorted out, I headed for shore before we got into really serious trouble.

I beached our skiff in a tiny cove in the lee of a wooded point and protected from the gale by a grove of tall, ancient spruce trees. I was very happy to be ashore, safe and sound, in such an ideal place to spend what promised to be a wild night. But when I informed my client that we would camp in the woods until the weather moderated, he went into a blue funk. To hear him rant one would have thought our situation most precarious and nearly hopeless! I wondered how this guy would behave in a really bad predicament!

I believe that every person ought to spend at least a few nights of his life in the wilderness before an open fire. If alone, it's a good time to philosophize, reflect, and to take one's inventory. Complex matters become simple when you're close to the earth. A campfire at night is one of the most cheerful and reassuring things I know of. In company with a good companion it's the perfect environment for swapping tales, practicing the basics of cooperation and sometimes cementing friendships. But with the man I had for a companion that night, it was a most unpleasant experience.

I selected a spot for our temporary campsite beneath a great spruce, so tall and sturdy-limbed that it shed the rain nearly as efficiently as a shingled roof. While I gathered a supply of wood and built a fire to keep us warm and comfortable during the night, my companion stumbled about loudly bemoaning our situation. He made not even token effort to rustle wood or gather moss for our beds. Instead he monotonously recited a litany of doom and gloom. Suppose the gale continued, he said, for a week or ten days or longer. We would starve! He wished he had never come to Alaska. Why hadn't I brought along a tent and stove and supplies for an emergency like this? Suppose the fire went out—could I start another one? Did I have enough matches and what would I do if they got wet and wouldn't light? What would I do if the skiff sank? Suppose we were attacked by a herd of man-eating grizzly bears. Suppose there was an earthquake. Finally he said that he was hungry.

"I gave you an apple a few hours ago," I said. "Eat that!"

"I already did," he answered.

When he began telling how unhappy his wife would be if he missed the appointment at Disneyland, I had all I could take for a while. So I sneaked away in the dark until I found a hollowed-out spot under a big tree. Here I snuggled down comfortably and slept very well until daylight.

When I returned to our campsite under the tall spruce, I discovered that my client had piled all of the wood I had gathered onto the fire. Then he had backed up too close to the blaze and burned the entire back out of his plastic raincoat.

When he unbuttoned the front the garment fell off his body in two pieces. This struck me as being comical and I laughed. But the dude failed to see the humor of the event. Now, he wailed, he had no raincoat to protect him from the elements, to add to all his other misfortunes.

Later that morning the wind calmed down and we were able to return to our cruiser. The cook had seen us coming and was frying bacon on the stove. When we came aboard, my hunter burst into the galley and began eating the partially cooked food right out of the pan, with all the nicety and finesse of a starving wolverine. He burned his fingers in the process and dropped a piece of greasy bacon on the cook's spotless galley floor. Then he shouted, "That's the last straw!" I doubt that my client knew just how nearly accurate that remark was!

Two days later, with time running out, my hunter shot a good representative grizzly—with just a bit of help from his guide, who was anxious to get the ordeal over with. As I was laying the bear out in position to be skinned and was honing my knife, my man was inspecting the dead grizzly critically. Just as I was about to make the primary cut from chin to tail, he announced, "I want the whole bear."

"I don't quite understand," I said. "You mean you want me to skin it out for a life-size museum mount?"

"No," he answered. "I want the whole bear, just like he is. The whole sunavabitchin' bear! I want it shipped to Texas where I can hang it up by the heels in front of the city hall where everybody in the county can see it! I want my picture taken in front of it, too. There's been a lot of people down there saying I wouldn't never get no bear in Alaska. Well, when they see this one hanging up by the heels and me standing in front of it, that'll show'em if I can kill a grizzly bear or not!"

I was flabbergasted. "You can't be serious," I said. "Look, there's no way this animal can be transported from where it lies here in this mud flat in Alaska, to Texas. This animal weighs at least seven hundred pounds. How are you and I going to drag it across this flat and get it aboard the boat? Tell me that!"

"Get a tractor," he replied. "Hire a gang of men. Charter a helicopter. Anyway, it's your problem—not mine. When we get aboard the cruiser, I'll show you a copy of the letter you wrote when we made a deal for this hunt. You wrote—I got the letter—that all I had to do was to shoot the bear and that you would do the rest. You said you would ship my trophy anywhere in the U.S.A. that I wanted it sent. That's what you *said* and I got it in writing! So get at it! I want the whole sunavabitchin' bear shipped to Texas."

I replaced my skinning knife into its sheath and sat on the dead bear to think. From the beginning I had decided that my client was neurotic, a bit wacky, pretty far out into left field at times. Now I wondered if this bozo wasn't actually mentally unbalanced, a refugee from the daffy castle, just plain crazy!

"It's getting late," I said. "Let's go aboard and have supper. I'll figure something out tomorrow."

My hunter was almost jovial at supper that evening. He had his trophy grizzly. Now all that remained was to have it shipped to Texas—"the whole sunavabitchin' bear." When the cook heard that statement, he looked long and hard at my client. "Jeez!" he said.

That night when I was sure all hands were sacked in and sleeping, I took a double-bitted ax, my knife and rifle and returned to the flat where we had killed the grizzly. Four hours later, I had skinned out the bear, fleshed and salted the pelt, dismembered the carcass, and dragged the parts into the adjoining river where they sank out of sight. I returned to the cruiser and was into my sleeping bag before anyone knew I had ever left.

After breakfast I returned to the meadow with my hunter. During the night the tide had come in and receded, effectively washing away the blood and disturbance I had left when I had earlier skinned the animal. When we reached the spot where the bear had been killed, my companion was puzzled. "Are you sure this is the place?" he asked.

"This is the place," I answered.

"But where's the bear?"

"Good question," I said, "Where *is* the bear! Something must have taken it."

"Something must have took it. Something must have took it!" he mimicked. "*What* took it? That's what I want to know—*what* took my bear?"

"Another good question," I said calmly. "Lots of strange things happen on Admiralty Island. Maybe a herd of bears came strolling by last night and carried your bear away to eat it. The Indians claim there are witches and evil spirits on this island that spend all their time figuring ways to louse up bear hunters—especially white bear hunters."

"To hell with the Indians and witches and evil spirits," shouted my companion in a crescendo. "What I want to know is what are you going to do about the bear I shot which ain't here— which something took?"

"Look!" I said. "You killed a trophy grizzly bear. You know and I know it. Something took it. So it's not your fault you have no bear to ship to Texas. Here's what I'm going to do. I'll get you your trophy grizzly—just as good or maybe even better than the one you shot. Then I'll ship your trophy to your home. You have my word. I promise. I guarantee it. Now the trip is over and I'll take you to town so you can meet your wife at Disneyland right on schedule." We shook hands and that evening we arrived in town. I think my client was happy that the hunt was finished. I certainly was!

A month later I shipped the salted pelt in a keg to the dude's home in Texas. In due time I received a short note from the mighty hunter saying that the hide arrived in good condition but *where was the rest of the bear*? Good question!

The Saga of
Sockless George

When I first came to the Territory of Alaska, there were a lot of individuals known as *characters*. They had interesting and descriptive names. There was Sea Lion Pete, Peg Leg Chris, Beer Barrel Benson, Rescue Pete, Wooden Wheel Jackson, Sea Gull Hansen, Poker Ole, Poor Ole, Hard-Working Paul, Handlogger Jackson, and Sockless George. There were others of course—many others—but these were a fair sampling of the characters who lived in the part of Alaska I knew more than half a century ago. The one I knew best and who was a standout above his peers was Sockless George.

Sockless George and I were partners on several seal hunting expeditions. If you ever want to know a man well, his faults, virtues, and idiosyncrasies, I would suggest that you make an extended wilderness hunting or trapping trip with him. Out there the strong become stronger, the wise wiser, and the fools more foolish.

Sockless George was barely literate, usually indigent and a member of no organization that I knew of. He had no wife, known relatives, Social Security card, or place of residence. He paid no taxes. He never voted, didn't know who was President of the United States, and didn't care. I have reason to believe he had never taken a bath or visited a barbershop. Most of the 1,800 residents of the community where I lived were not aware of his existence. Certainly none of the citizens who lived in white houses up on the hill ever invited him to dinner or had him as a house guest. I doubt that Sockless George knew much if anything about his ancestry. His skin was the color of Hudson Bay tea or muskeg water in the late summer. His hair was coarse, straight and black. He had dark, bright eyes and his vision was about equal to an ordinary man using 4x binoculars. He might have been forty or fifty or sixty years of age. He was a wonderful partner to have out in the wilderness when life was sometimes a matter of survival under most adverse conditions. And he was the best seal hunter I ever knew in my long career as a professional in Alaska.

It was because of an accident or miscalculation that I became acquainted with this character with the euphonious name. It was in March (1940, I believe) when I was hunting seals for bounty near the mouth of the Stikene River. At the time my financial situation was somewhat worse than bad. Times were tough, and I had a wife and infant son to support. My only source of income was from hunting and trapping. In those days you swam or sank, and I was doing my best not to sink.

One evening I rowed my skiff into a small cove where there was a freshwater creek. Seals like to visit such places, especially at dawn in the winter. I pitched my tent and set up the Yukon stove and chimney near the edge of the woods. Then I moved my outfit ashore and into the tent. There wasn't much to move. All I had were a couple of blankets, a water bucket, an ax, a box of grub and my single-shot .22 Hornet rifle with ammunition. The only fuel available at this campsite was green spruce, which burns nearly as badly as wet cottonwood, which is practically incombustible.

The weather had been remarkably mild for that time of the year, but that night the wind shifted to the north and a wicked

70

gale blew down from the glaciers on the mainland. When the fire burned out in my stove, the cold crept in. Frost gathered inside the tent and the water bucket froze. Though I was fully clothed, I shivered beneath my blankets and was thoroughly miserable. It was cold!

At the first hint of dawn, I arose and began trying to start a fire in the stove with green spruce shavings. After a great deal of effort I finally managed to coax along a fire that hissed, sputtered and smoked but gave forth very little heat. I had about forty pounds of seal blubber in my skiff which I planned to use for wolf bait. I packed up the entire mess and piled it atop the weak flame in the stove. Presently the fat began to melt and oil dripped down onto the wood. The fire began burning more vigorously. I held my hands over the stove and enjoyed the warmth. Frost on the tent walls started to melt. I set the frozen water bucket on the stove to make coffee water. Then, when the stove began puffing like a steam locomotive, I went outside to perform morning chores and see if any seals had appeared at the creek mouth.

A few minutes later, when I turned back toward my tent, I could hardly believe what I saw. Black, ugly smoke was pouring from the chimney. The canvas surrounding it was beginning to blacken and burn. When I threw open the flap of the tent I recoiled from the blast of heat that struck me. I stepped back, drew in a long, deep breath of air, and dashed back inside the tent. I grabbed my blankets and the grub box and dragged them into the open. By now all of the tent near the stove was aflame.

Standing out there on that lonely shore in the frigid cold, watching my tent burn and the white hot stove and chimney collapse, was one of the low spots of my Alaskan career. All that I had left of my outfit was an unseaworthy skiff, a pair of hand-hewn oars, a cheap rifle and two blankets. Even the few seal scalps I had collected on the trip had been destroyed in the fire. It looked like my bounty hunting had been finished for the season.

71

Sadly, I ate a handful of raw oatmeal and chewed on a scrap of raw seal blubber. Then I put the box of grub, my two blankets and rifle in the skiff and started rowing toward home. I had no money in the bank, I owned less than three dollars cash and my credit was shaky. Life in the far north looked bleak that day.

After resting a couple of days in town, I began feeling more optimistic. Spring was coming. Soon the weather would improve. The days were lengthening at the rate of five minutes a day. If I could somehow acquire a suitable skiff and pick up a piece of canvas to make a shelter, I could continue my bounty hunting. It wouldn't be the first time I had survived for a considerable period in the wilderness, sleeping in the open and cooking on a campfire. What I needed most was a good skiff. Someone told me that Sockless George had an extra skiff. Maybe I could borrow it.

I found Sockless George holding an impromptu open house behind Sing Lee Alley and the waterfront. He was standing behind a 2 x 12 plank laid between two buoy kegs. On the plank were several gallon jugs containing various brands of cheap, fortified wine. Gathered about was an assemblage of individuals who would have delighted any modern day social worker or bureaucrat working on a program for the betterment of the underprivileged minorities of the nation. Most of the revelers were in various stages of inebriation. The only person excepting Sockless George that I knew by name was Hard-Working Paul. Though Paul had never been known to hold any job longer than twenty-four hours, he had an uncanny ability to sense where free potables were being dispensed. Sockless George presided over the revelry, acting as bartender, confidant, peacemaker and—when sporadic fisticuffs erupted—referee. When a jug became empty, he replaced it with a full one. He was truly the life of the party and the most popular man present. Those who dispense largesse usually are popular while their money lasts.

When Sockless George spotted me, he motioned me over.

"Have some wine," he said. "Make you feel good. Settles the stomach. Keeps the worms down, too!"

I have never been a wine drinker, particularly the two-dollar-a-gallon variety. However, rather than risk offending this man with whom I had hoped to reach an agreement pertaining to a skiff I needed and wanted to borrow, I lifted a jug to my mouth and took a couple of swallows. It was vile stuff—even worse than I had expected. I could well imagine that if one had intestinal worms they wouldn't survive long when the wine caught up with them. I set the jug down and coughed. There were tears in my eyes. Sockless George reached for the jug, raised it to his lips and took a long, slow pull. Setting the crock back down on the plank, he blinked his eyes rapidly. Then he expelled his breath with a loud whooshing sound like a grizzly bear makes when startled. "Gee whiz," he said, "dat's good stuff. I'll be glad when it's all gone so I can get back to my camp hunting seals again."

"I know what you mean," I answered. "I'd like to get back hunting seals, too. But I need a skiff. Mine's about done for. I spend as much time bailing as I do rowing. I hear you have an extra skiff. I'd like to borrow it. In fact I'd like to buy it as soon as I'm able. Where is the skiff? I'd like to have a look at it."

Sockless George pointed toward the mainland miles away. Then he made a wide sweeping gesture with his arm, encompassing an area of about one thousand square miles. "Over there," he said.

Two days later I was with George in his skiff rowing toward his camp in an ice-filled fiord where he assured me "there was everyt'ing a man needs." I carried my two blankets, a few spare clothes, a rifle and a box of ammunition. Sockless George had no baggage except his .22 Hornet rifle and a box of fifty cartridges. We had no grub.

Though my partner was certainly older than I and complained of suffering from an "overhang," from the drinking, he performed his fair share of rowing and we made good progress.

Since he had repeatedly assured me that his camp was well-provisioned, in my mind's eye I had a picture of a snug, comfortable cabin in the wilderness. There would be shelves and lockers filled with canned goods and staples—beans, flour, rice, oatmeal, dried fruit—all the foods considered necessary to men who work hard and scorn luxuries. Of course, there would be a big woodpile to supply the stove. Possibly the cabin would have a stone fireplace. There would be a couple of bunks, table, chairs, and cooking pots and pans.

Early that evening we pulled into a small cove where there was a gravel beach near a clear creek. We secured our skiff and George led the way up a kind of a trail that went toward the timber. I followed. In less than two minutes we came to an opening in the woods. There was a circle of blackened stones that was obviously a campfire site and nearby was a five-gallon gasoline can with a wire handle hanging from the limb of a spruce tree. An ax was stuck into a stump. There was hardly any other sign that a human being had ever been there. This was the camp of Sockless George, where there was "everyt'ing a man needs."

"Gee whiz," said George, "it's good to be back in camp again where a man can be comfortable. By golly! Already my overhang is gone."

It had been a long day, we had worked hard, and I was hungry. I wondered if perhaps Sockless George had a cache of food stashed away out of the reach of prowling bears and wolverines. I should have known better. "Time to eat," said my companion. "Tide's out and the table's set."

He removed the empty gasoline can from where it hung on a limb and we went to the nearby beach. At the edge of the receding tide, George started to dig in the gravel with an old tire iron. It didn't take us long to gather a good supply of white-shelled butter clams, the kind we call "steamers" in Alaska. In the process, we discovered many creatures that crawled, squirmed, wriggled and squirted. These, too, were added to the collection of clams in the can. When we had enough bounty of the sea to supply a dozen or more dainty eaters, we started a fire at our "camp." In a few minutes the mess was sufficiently steamed. We spread the contents of the can onto a large flat rock, and it was each man for himself.

I'm quite sure that persons of refinement and dainty eating habits would have been revolted at the mere sight of what George and I dined on that night. The clams were really delicious and even the various crawling and squirming creatures that had been cooked were not at all bad. Certainly they were different! After supper, the food that was left was put back in the can which was again hung from a limb. "Gee whiz! I feel good," said Sockless George. Then, fully clothed, he crawled under a giant spruce into a moss-filled hollow, which might once have been a bear's den, and disappeared. My seal hunting partner had retired for the night!

I spread my blankets on a relatively level piece of mossy ground under the towering boughs of the same tree George had burrowed under. I could hear the booming of the glacier at the head of the inlet when icebergs broke off. The wind moaned softly in the trees and I heard a seal talking out on the water. I was wondering what we would do if the weather turned really cold when I fell asleep.

I was starting a fire the next morning to warm up our breakfast when I noticed the moss under the big spruce begin to move. Then I saw my partner emerge. He was covered with moss and debris and looked very primitive. I wouldn't have been greatly surprised if he had growled. When he stood erect, he shook himself like a bear does when it comes out of a creek. He ran his fingers through his hair to clear it of moss. Then he breathed deeply and expelled the air with the loud whooshing sound I was becoming familiar with. "By golly!" he said, "I feel good." It seemed I'd heard that line before.

After breakfast, we started hunting seals. At that period of my career I really thought that I was an expert seal hunter. In my opinion I was as good as anyone and better than most. After a few days with Sockless George, I changed my opinion. I realized that I was a novice and George was a master. There were professional seal hunters in the area who killed more seals than the sockless one and collected more bounties. But these pros had the finest of equipment—powerboats, cabins strategically located, ample supplies, plenty of conventional food and, most important, they had the finest of rifles and telescopic sights.

The harbor or so-called hair seal of southeastern Alaska, on which there was a bounty in those days, must be the most difficult of all living targets. Shooting woodchucks, by comparison, is easy. The only part of the seal that shows is the top of the head, which is about the size of half a cantaloupe. The animal is usually moving, frequently bobbing with the waves and seldom remains visible more than a few seconds. Whenever seals are being hunted they become extremely wary. They stay way out there at the extreme range of the finest rifles and even beyond that. The rifle most favored by the professionals was a heavy barreled target weapon, like a .220 Swift, that was deadly accurate at three hundred yards, or even more. These rifles were equipped with ten- or twelve-power telescopic sights that were nearly as long as the rifle's barrel. Many hunters used hand-loaded ammunition for better accuracy. Even with such superb rifles, the very best of the professionals didn't kill every seal they fired at. Not by a long shot!

Sockless George hunted seals, successfully, with a light-barreled, single-shot .22 Hornet with *iron sights.* It's effective range was about one hundred and fifty yards. By any standard such a rifle was inadequate for seal shooting. It was positively primitive. It was like hunting Kodiak bear with a .44-40! But what George lacked in shooting equipment, he more than made up for in expertise. If it's possible for a man to think like a seal, George was that man. Time and time again I have seen him accurately anticipate a seal's movement when it was swimming under the water and out of sight. At such times he would be aiming his rifle at almost the exact spot where the seal's head appeared above the surface and get off a shot before the creature was aware of our presence. I won't say he was the best offhand shot I've known. But I have never known any other person who shot so well from a moving boat while standing upright.

And Sockless George knew all the tricks. Perhaps there were one or two he invented. Like all highly intelligent animals, seals are very curious creatures. They seem unable to resist investigating any unusual movement or strange object. My partner relied frequently on this facet of seal behavior. Sometimes when the animals were staying far out of range, he would expose himself on a prominent point of land where he was in full view and move about to attract attention of any seal in the water.

At times he would rig up a pole with his shirt tied onto it and wave it like a flag. It was only a very wise and experienced seal that could resist coming in close to investigate *that!*

Late one evening when the weather was so mild that we heard an occasional blue grouse hoot back in the hills, my partner performed an action that I would have scarcely believed had I not been a witness. We were sitting on a glacier-scoured point of land, watching for seals. There weren't many around and those few we saw were too far out. George laid his rifle down and remarked, "I show you something." Then he produced a harmonica from one of the pockets of his jacket. It was a cheap, dime-store instrument, old and battered. He put it to his mouth and began playing it. The sounds that came forth were certainly unlike any conventional music I've ever heard. Perhaps it wasn't music at all. It was weird, haunting—strangely melodious. Perhaps Cro-Magnon man made such sounds to the cave bear and other creatures of the wild to soothe them. Twice that evening seals came to within fifty feet of us and raised their bodies half out of the water. Each time I was ready and killed the seal with one shot into the neck. When we retrieved the seals, in each case George bent down low over the body and said

77

something in a low voice. It was like a religious ceremony. It would have been improper to ask him what he said.

Sockless George was by no means garrulous. But some evenings when the weather was pleasant and the hunting had gone well that day, he would reminisce. He liked to tell of his trip to Seattle. To George, Seattle was a far-away, never-never place. It was like Paris or Mecca or Shangri-La is to some people. "Gee whiz," he would say, "the buildings is higher than dese trees. My goodness! And all dose people. T'ousands of dem! Dere's so many you keep bumping into dem all the time."

"How long were you in Seattle?" I asked.

"Only a few days." he said. "I lost all my money. I got pickpocked."

"You got pickpocked?" I inquired.

"Sure t'ing. Someone pickpock me."

"So what did you do?"

"I borrowed a skiff from someone and rowed back to Alaska," Sockless George said.

I wondered how many living men were capable of rowing a skiff from Puget Sound to Alaska without food, supplies or equipment. But then I remembered that there weren't many men like Sockless George to whom the table was set when the tide was out!

"Did you ever return the skiff you borrowed?" I asked.

"Not yet," said my seal hunting partner. "I been too busy. I never got time."

Another tale my partner told me once, and once only, which intrigued me greatly, was about the rock he picked up on the side of a mountain. He said it was about the size of his fist and was heavy like a piece of lead. And it was laced and criss-crossed with wire gold. He told me the rock was laying out in the open on the surface of the ground just above timberline. He said he had wandered about in the area the rest of the day but found no other rocks like it. When I asked him where this place was he ᵢade the same sweeping gesture with his arm he had made when I asked him the location of his skiff, while we were in town.

"What did you do with the rock?" I asked.

"Well," said George, "by golly, it was a good heavy rock, so I tied it up in a piece of fish net and used it for an anchor for my skiff. Then one day I lost it overboard."

"You used a rock that you could see the gold in for an anchor?" I asked incredulously.

"Sure t'ing," said Sockless George. "It was just da right size for an anchor and it was heavy too. Gee whiz! Dat's the heaviest rock I ever seen!"

I do not recall how many days we hunted seals on that first trip—fifteen or sixteen at a guess. We had a fair collection of scalps and a few of the better hides. Also our supply of ammunition was nearly exhausted. It was time to return to town. In spite of, or perhaps because of, our steady diet of sea food, kelp and seal liver, I felt wonderfully fit and healthy. At night, lying on a bed of moss and rolled up in my two blankets, I slept as relaxed and as soundly as a cat. It was a joy to be living and I wouldn't have traded places with any other person on earth.

Once we were clear of the icebergs enroute to town I asked George regarding the whereabouts of the skiff I had asked to borrow. "Gee whiz!" he said, "is that all you can talk about, borrowing a skiff? Some other time I show it to you. Now, I'm in a hurry to get to town."

During the next several years I made other trips with Sockless George. I enjoyed being with this strange man and learned much about hunting and wilderness survival. Many times I have put his philosophy of the table being set when the tide is out to practical use.

One fall day George left town, probably suffering from an "overhang," rowing his skiff toward his camp where there was everything a man needs. He never returned. The authorities declared that he left an estate of "less than a hundred dollars," as I recall. I'm sure they were right. I don't suppose a dozen men

79

in all Alaska were aware that he was gone. He died unwept, unhonored, and unsung, as the poet wrote.

Many years later, toward the end of my Alaskan career, I visited our old seal-hunting camp. The same rusty five-gallon gasoline can with the wire handle hung from the limb of the ancient spruce. His ax was still stuck in a log. Still visible was the circle of camp fire stones where we had cooked our food and I had listened to the tales Sockless George had told me. I looked under the big tree where George had burrowed in and slept so many nights, winter and summer. I felt a certain sadness as I wandered about our old hunting grounds. But in a way I was glad my old partner was gone. He hadn't lived to see Alaska change. He didn't live to see it become a place where a man's word was no longer inviolate, where cabins were vandalized, and people locked the doors of their home. Sockless George wouldn't have understood those things.

Photographic Souvenirs

A PORTFOLIO

An Admiralty Island vista. Whenever I come back here, the problems and woes of civilization seem remote, unimportant.

A Sitka blacktail doe and her fawn were crossing a gravel bar as I snapped this. Unfortunately, clear-cut logging operations on national forest land are rapidly shrinking the habitat of these deer and other animals.

Here's how I remember Admiralty Island in summer.

In the subarctic twilight, the trees in the foreground are silhouettes, as black as their mirrored images on the water's surface, while the forests in the distance are still glowing in a golden light.

I posed for this photo, holding a rod and a fresh-caught trout, while participating in the filming of a documentary, *Cheechako*, back in the summer of 1954. The location was Kadake Creek on Kuiu Island, and at that time the creek provided fabulous trout and salmon fishing.

A client took this shot of me as I worked on a grizzly hide that weighed at least a hundred and fifty pounds. Even though I'm leaning over in the picture, maybe you can gauge the bear's size by mine; I stand five feet ten inches tall. From nose to hind pads, that hanging hide was nearly twelve feet long. It was shot by a doctor from Ohio, in October of 1961 at Pybus Bay, Admiralty. We estimated this grizzly's live weight at nearly fourteen hundred pounds.

84

Here I am with Richard Burton at Petersburg, Alaska, during the filming of *Ice Palace*. I was hired by the filmmakers as a guide and consultant. In case you're in doubt about which one is Richard Burton, I'm on the left in this snapshot.

A young bald eagle in flight. Many years ago, I hunted these birds for the one-dollar bounty that was then paid by the Territory of Alaska. How little I knew in those days, how little I could predict. How little we all knew. Today it's unlawful to possess even a feather of an eagle.

A mature bald eagle on the ground. Fortunately, these birds remain a common sight in the upper Northwest, but there's reason to wonder about the future.

Wild salmon berries. These edible fruits look a lot like raspberries, but wild currents are my favorites and blueberries are what the bears like best. Alaska's wilderness provides the traveler with a profusion of natural, tasty, nutritious snacks.

The beaches of southeastern Alaska are a trove of clams, a treat not only for the human wayfarer but for eagles, ravens, crows, gulls, mink, otters, and wolves. Strangely, however, the bears ignore this rich source of protein.

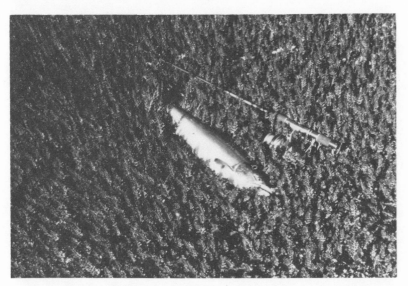

A few minutes of sport will furnish a man with plenty of salmon for one day, and there will be tidbits left over for the birds as well.

Salmon jumping in a pool on Admiralty Island Creek. This little pool holds hundreds of trout as well as salmon. From the spot where I took the picture, I watched many grizzlies during the years when I guided hunters.

Here are the falls on Admiralty Island Creek. This marks the end of the run for spawning salmon, for no fish can get above the falls.

Grizzly tracks sunk deep into the mud near the water's edge. The vegetation is sedge, a favorite food of bears in the springtime.

This black bear was so close it heard my shutter click above the sound of the water.

A trophy-size male grizzly, fishing in a salmon creek on Admiralty.

The hunter with this black bear is the late Lew Bulgrin, president of Badger Shooter's Supply Company of Owen, Wisconsin. Lew was a wonderful friend, a fine hunter, and an exceptional marksman. He made three hunts with me, and on those hunts he took three grizzlies and six black bears. To kill those nine bears, he fired exactly nine bullets.

This is a prime spring black bear, killed by Fred Huntington of Oroville, California. The pelt squared out at about seven feet four inches, and black bears seldom grow much larger. A sportsman might hunt for a lifetime without seeing a black bear like this one.

Here's Eastern Airlines pilot Earl McKenzie with the fine grizzly he took. Stalking grizzlies in this kind of habitat can be hazardous. Even when hit by a well-placed shot from a powerful rifle, a bear may not go down or stay down. This one had to be trailed after the first shot, and he was finished at nearly point-blank range in heavy cover.

My hatted companion in this picture, taken in August of 1964, was Frank Dufresne, and it turned out to be the last photograph of Frank. He helped to establish the Alaska Game Commission, and he's also remembered as the author of several books. His last fine book was the one entitled *No Room for Bears*. I was proud to be Frank Dufresne's friend.

I wish I'd been closer when I took this snapshot, because the man in this tidal meadow, aiming at a distant Admiralty grizzly, was far from a typical client. He was one of the century's greatest hunting writers, the late Jack O'Connor.

Adult trumpeter swans—pure white birds with a ten-foot wingspan and a call that, to some of us, is like celestial music. It comforts me to reflect that I took this picture in 1983. My hope is that generations of Alaskans yet unborn may see these noble creatures in their wilderness habitat.

Here's what some people call progress. It's a timber operation on national forest land.

The death of a salmon stream on Admiralty Island. In 1930 this watershed had an estimated run of 2,950,000 salmon, according to the U.S. Bureau of Fisheries. What you see here is the tragic result of logging methods condoned and even supervised by the U.S. Forest Service. Putting aside esthetic and spiritual values for a moment, think of the inestimable economic loss when a resource like this is squandered. Think of a yearly salmon run that numbered nearly three million fish. And then, yes, I guess we'd all better think about the esthetic and spiritual values, the loss of which can't be counted or measured. I have to wonder how much can ever be restored, how much more will be wasted, how much saved?

Trapping Can Be Ticklish

I began trapping when I was nine years old, not so much by choice as by necessity. We were living in Clatsop County in northwestern Oregon, which at that time was still a frontier. As on any frontier, everyone seemed to have enough, but nobody, at least by modern standards, could have been considered affluent. On the whole we were as well off or better off than our neighbors. My father worked for the army at nearby Fort Stevens at a salary of forty-five dollars a month. In addition to this princely income, we had a Jersey cow that produced an astonishing quantity of cream-rich milk each day, a flock of chickens that laid large brown eggs, and a garden where we grew all the vegetables we could use plus a surplus to give our less fortunate neighbors. Yes, we were prosperous, and that prosperity might have continued longer than it did except for one thing.

My father was a gambler—a compulsive gambler, I believe. Each payday he would play poker with the soldiers from the fort. Dad understood the odds and probabilities better than most of those with whom he played. He was also skillful at manipulating the cards. Whenever conditions were favorable he practiced such chicaneries as false cutting, dealing from the bottom, and switching decks. Because he was dexterous, studious, and amoral, my father usually won money when he played poker. But Dad had a weakness. At more or less regular intervals and for months at a time, he would drink too much whiskey. As a result he would lose his skills and judgment and do foolish things such as drawing to inside straights, opening pots with a small pair, and betting when he should have passed. There came a period in the fall of 1915 when there was no money in the house and my sister and I went barefoot even after the rains began. Had it not been for the fish and game that was available in addition to what our chickens, cow, and garden produced, things might have been awkward! About this time I learned that muskrat hides were selling for twenty five cents and a mink pelt could bring as much as a dollar and fifty cents. I decided to go trapping.

I learned the basics of trapping mink and muskrats and caring for the pelts from a strange old man who lived alone in a shack at the edge of a marsh near town. No one knew much about him. We occasionally came to town to buy a few staples, which he paid for in gold coin. It was rumored that he had been a wicked man in earlier times and that he had robbed banks and had done other terrible things. Perhaps these rumors had some basis of fact, but I think he was merely a lonely old man who longed for companionship. When I visited him he made me welcome and gave me pieces of deer jerky and salt pork to chew on. He taught me other valuable things, too, such as how to walk quietly in the woods and the art of honing a knife. Today, in the twilight of my life, I marvel that so few youths know how to walk quietly or put a keen edge on a skinning knife. Most of the young people that I know aren't interested in such matters.

Within hiking distance of our home were many sloughs, ponds, creeks, marshes, and estuaries. All had goodly populations of muskrats and a few mink. I purchased eighteen No. 1½ steel traps on credit from Holbrook's store, and my career as a trapper began. What I lacked in experience and expertise I compensated for in enthusiasm and dedication. I caught a fair amount of fur that winter—enough in fact to help out with household expenses and to buy my mother a new dress and my sister and me each a pair of shoes. Dad was impressed, and that spring he stopped drinking whiskey and began winning money once more when he played poker. Again we were prosperous.

When I moved to Alaska, trapping was an important segment of the economy. Large areas and whole villages of Eskimos and Indians depended almost entirely on trapping fox, beaver, mink, marten, and otter for their livelihood. There were no food stamps or welfare programs in those days. A poor trapping season in the arctic regions could mean hardship for many people. In some instances it has meant disaster—even starvation. In southern Alaska where I settled, trapping was a way of life for hundreds of residents. Each winter when jobs were scarce or nonexistent, these men went into the wilderness to harvest the annual crop of fur. I was one of these. I could not have survived those first few years in the northland had I not trapped.

The summer of 1942 was a particularly unprofitable one for me. I shipped on a salmon fishing boat with high hopes of making a winter stake. Right from the beginning, things went bad. Though there was a fair run of salmon that year, we always seemed to be at the wrong place at the wrong time. When the salmon were running strongly to the north we were south, and when the fish moved south we traveled northward. When we finally caught up with the fish, we ripped our seine badly on a reef. We anchored in a bay and lost three days of fishing time while repairing the damage. At the height of the season when everyone was catching fish we developed engine trouble. We were towed to town for overhaul and lost a full week of a short season. Finally our skipper got drunk and we lost more valuable fishing time. When we settled up that fall my share of the gross stock wasn't sufficient to pay even current and overdue bills. I divided what cash I had between the grocer and landlord, promising to pay more when I was able. With snow already in the foothills and with a long winter imminent, I was dead broke and had a wife and child to support.

Late in November, I assembled an outfit consisting of what traps I had, two blankets, a cooking pot, my .300 Savage, ammunition, an ax, skinning knife, and a few pounds of rice, beans, flour, and some spare clothing. I had no tent or even a piece of canvas for shelter. With this skimpy outfit lashed to a packboard, I hiked overland across Kuprenof Island until I reached Duncan Canal—a long inlet that nearly bisects the island.

I built a lean-to, cut a supply of wood and shot two deer. I skinned the deer and hung the butchered parts on the limbs of trees where they would remain fresh a long while. One of the hides I used for a ground cloth and the other to cover my blankets. If there is any better insulation than a deerskin I don't know what it is. With my winter camp established I laid out two traplines—one to the east and the other in the opposite direction.

Each morning before daylight and again when darkness came I would build a small fire for cooking and warmth. I made certain that my fires were completely extinguished during daylight so that no wisp of smoke would rise above the trees and betray the location of my camp. Because I had no skiff I had to walk ten miles to cover a five-mile trapline. When the tides were unfavorable I had to travel even farther, sloshing as much as a mile up and back down a flooding slough for a net gain of a few hundred feet.

I had picked a poor area to trap, and fur was not plentiful. Some days I would catch a mink or two but as often I would come back to my bleak camp at night, cold, weary and discouraged without a single piece of fur to show for my effort. There came a cold snap in January when the temperature at night would go down to near zero. My traps froze and became inoperable. For about a week my life became a matter of survival. I remember mornings when I crawled out of my blankets, stiff and numb with the cold, to chop meat from a frozen deer carcass with my ax, wondering how much more I could endure. At last the weather moderated and I resumed trapping, but my cache of furs, which I hung in the lee of a spruce, remained pitifully small.

One night late in February I awoke with excruciating pain in the region of my left kidney. In all my life I have never experienced such agony. I thought I was dying, and perhaps I was. When daylight came I discovered that I was passing a substance that appeared to be a mixture of coarse sand and blood in my urine. I had no appetite and vomited up even the water I drank. After resting a day, I started hiking overland toward home, packing only my blankets, rifle, and furs. I almost didn't make it. Back in town the local doctor diagnosed my trouble as kidney stones. He gave me sedatives and advised that I take things easy for a while. I sold my furs and divided the cash I received among my creditors. That was a tough winter. Had I not been a trapper, we might not have made it through until spring.

The Territory of Alaska had trapping regulations, but due to the vastness of the area and the paucity of wardens, enforcement was spotty. Also, the courts were inclined to give light sentences to violators. However, there were two unwritten laws for which the penalty for violation was sometimes swift, sudden death. One of these unwritten laws was: *THOU SHALT NOT TRESPASS ON ANOTHER TRAPPER'S TERRITORY.* The other was: *THOU SHALT NOT TAKE FUR FROM ANOTHER MAN'S TRAP.* I knowingly and willfully violated each of these laws and consider myself fortunate to have lived to relate the tale.

At the conclusion of the war with Japan the country was suddenly flooded with money and the price of fur rose to unheard-of heights. All over Alaska the regular professional

101

trappers plus a host of *cheechakos* went into the wilderness to share the wealth. It was almost like a gold rush.

In the winter of 1945–1946 I formed a partnership with a man I shall refer to as Tom although that was not his name. He was tall, lean, short-tempered, immensely powerful and one of the best trappers in southeastern Alaska. For various reasons we were late leaving town, and when we reached the area we had planned to work we found that it was practically saturated with trappers who had arrived earlier. After much searching we finally located a limited area still unoccupied near the southern extremity of Kuprenof Island. Here, a few hundred yards south of a large creek that drained the interior of the island, we built a cabin and laid in a supply of wood for winter. All of the land north and west of the creek mentioned above was traditional Indian trapping ground. For generations, as far back as the Russian occupation, the Indians had lived and trapped on this land. Only a very foolish or reckless white man would set traps here. Some of those who did invade this traditional Indian country never returned to civilization. They simply disappeared. I never knew an Indian who professed to have the least knowledge of what happened to those bold but unwise venturers.

The cabin we built was a primitive affair. It was constructed of poles and hand-split spruce shakes. It had a door but no window. We spread beach gravel for a floor and our stove was a gasoline drum cut in half with a piece of sheet iron for a top. Except when we lit our gasoline lantern, our dwelling was as dark as a tomb. But it was dry and warm and infinitely better than living in a tent or sleeping in the open.

We spread out fourteen dozen traps and it didn't take us long to pick up most of the fur on the ground available. One evening while we were attending to the pelts taken that day, Tom suddenly said, "We need more ground to trap. Ain't enough here for two men. Few more days and we'll have our ground pretty well cleaned out and it's not even Christmas yet. We got to move. We need more ground to trap if we're going to make a season."

"That's right," I said, "but where are we going to move? Where are we going to find more ground that hasn't already been taken up?"

"We're going to move into Indian country," Tom said. "There's no other place to go."

I finished putting a mink pelt on a stretching board and hung it on a rafter to dry. "Indians ain't going to like that", I said. Tom bristled up. He looked mean as a wolverine. "Hell with the Indians," he said. "They don't own this land. They got no more right to trap here that we have. There ain't no law says they do. Tomorrow morning we start moving in on them."

"I don't like it," I said. "Sometimes these Indians play rough."

"What's the matter," sneered Tom, "you afraid of a few Indians? They play rough, we play rough too. Tomorrow morning we start moving in on them. We need more ground!"

So the next day we began picking up our traps and setting them deep into Indian country north of the creek. Whenever we found an Indian's trap we made it inoperable either by carefully placing a spruce cone under the pan or sprinkling a bit of outboard motor fuel over the trap. Several days we labored mightily, laying out miles of trapline. Right from the start we began taking fur. Though we did not see any Indians, I had the most uncomfortable feeling that we were being watched. I considered the possibility that we might be bushwhacked, and I started carrying my rifle.

One morning, an hour before dawn, while I was cooking breakfast and Tom was mending a pair of trousers he had snagged the previous day, the door of our cabin opened suddenly and four Indians walked in. None of them carried weapons. For a few moments they stood silently, gazing speculatively at us, at the furs hanging from the rafters and at my rifle and shotgun suspended on pegs driven in the wall along my bunk. For what seemed a long while no word was spoken and the only sound was the crackling of wood in our stove. Then one of our visitors who wore a bright yellow cap and seemed to be the chief man spoke. "You fellows been trapping on our ground," he said. "Now you move out. You don't move, there's going to be trouble."

My partner dropped the trousers he had been mending and stood up. He looked formidable and dangerous. "What do you mean there's going to be trouble?" he said in his bass voice. "What kind of trouble? If there's going to be trouble, let's have it right now!"

I don't think the Indians expected this kind of reaction. Morally they were in the right and physically we were outnumbered. Briefly, they talked among themselves in a language, which neither Tom nor I understood. Finally they looked once more at the fur hanging from the rafters and at us. Then they opened the door as quietly as they had entered. The last to leave was Yellow Cap. As he stepped out he turned and faced us. "You move," he said, "or there's going to be trouble. Very bad trouble!" Then he closed the door, and I heard the wooden latch click shut.

I finished cooking breakfast and filled our two mugs with coffee. "These people mean business," I said.

"Naw," said Tom, "they're bluffing. They're trying to scare us. I know these Indians. Look, today's December 22. Indians always go to their village for Christmas and don't never come back until after New Year. By that time we'll have their ground, and ours too, picked pretty clean. We got nothing to worry about. Them people that was here this morning are probably on their way to the village right now."

"Hope you're right," I said.

"Damn right I'm right," said Tom. "I know Indians better than they know themselves."

Of all the sins that beset mankind, greed is perhaps the deadliest. Because we were greedy we continued to trap ever deeper into forbidden Indian country. The weather continued mild and we were reaping a harvest of fur. Shortly after Christmas it snowed several inches. We saw plenty of tracks of mink, otter, deer, and even wolves but nary a sign of another human being. Tom was right—the Indians had left. Still I was uneasy. All the while I traveled and tended my traps I carried a rifle loaded, cocked and with the safety latch on. Tom seemed amused at my caution.

Then one night it turned cold and the snow crusted. Our traps had to be dug out and reset. For a day or two we wouldn't take much fur. The next morning when Tom sized up the situation he announced that he would take the skiff, a few traps and a light outfit and investigate some of the small offshore islands that might have been overlooked by other trappers that winter. He said that he would be gone three or four days while I stayed at our base camp and tended the regular trap line. Before leaving that morning he remarked, "You aren't afraid to stay here alone, are you?"

What do you say when your partner asks if you're afraid?

"Hell, no!" I answered. "I'm not afraid. You go look over them islands. I'll be here when you come back." I tried to sound convincing but the fact is I didn't relish being alone and running a trap line on ground claimed by Indians who had warned us to leave or there would be trouble. *Bad trouble.* All that day I worked hard at digging out and resetting traps. There was no reason to suppose that the Indians had not left the area, but I was uneasy, watchful and apprehensive. It was good to be back in the cabin that evening snug, warm and safe. After supper, I skinned and stretched a couple of mink I had taken that day, attended to the usual chores, cut dry kindling for the morning fire, turned out the lantern and sacked in. The darkness inside the cabin was absolute.

Sometime after midnight I suddenly awoke. Close by and outside the wall where my bunk was located I could hear an ominous sound. Someone was walking on the crusted snow.

Crunch, crunch, crunch—stealthily, purposefully and deliberatively. I could hear whoever was out there make his way around the corner of the cabin toward the door. There was an Indian out there. I was sure of it and I was scared. The skin over my forehead was tightening and my heart was beating rapidly. I removed the shotgun from pegs on the wall. It was a 12-gauge trombone-action and fully loaded. I slipped the safety off and, clad only in my underwear and socks, eased out of the bunk onto the gravel floor. Just outside the cabin door the crunching on the snow abruptly ceased. Holding my gun at the ready, I waited. It was dark inside the cabin but I knew that outside it was nearly as light as day, what with the moon shining on the snow. The moment the latch lifted and the door swung open I would shoot at whoever stood outside. At point-blank range I could hardly miss.

In the silence and darkness I waited for what seemed a long while but in reality must have been a very short time. At last the waiting and indecision became unbearable. Moving ever so carefully and taking short steps, I approached the door, lifted the latch and swung it wide open. There, a few feet away stood a small deer, hardly more than a fawn, staring at me with eyes as large as two saucers. The situation was so ludicrous that I nearly laughed aloud. I poked the little animal with the barrel of the gun. It gave forth with a bleat and minced over to the edge of the woods where it stood a moment looking at me in utter fascination.

After that experience I ceased to worry about the Indians. I didn't carry my rifle when tending the trapline. When my partner returned to the cabin we picked up all our traps and returned to town. We sold our fur for about three thousand dollars. It had been a profitable and interesting season. For all that, never again have I ever trespassed on another trapper's territory. Quite frankly, sportsmanship and morality haven't been the primary considerations; it just ain't healthy to horn in on another trapper. It's bad for one's longevity.

Afognak Island lies north of and adjacent to Kodiak Island. Fifty years ago there was a tiny native village on the southern extremity of Afognak—the only permanent habitation in an otherwise trackless wilderness. It was into this remote village that I wandered one cold snowy day late in December, 1931. I was ill prepared and poorly equipped to survive the winter in that bleak, inhospitable sub-arctic wilderness. Everything I owned was contained in a canvas sea bag. I had no proper footwear, only a single suit of underwear and no money. I was a total stranger in a native village where the only other white man was a Russian Orthodox priest, and we had little in common. I don't know what would have happened to me that winter had not a native family taken me in and treated me as though I were one of them. They gave me food, shelter, and clothing. In return, I cut wood, shot seals for food, and behaved myself.

After awhile I grew restless and wearied of the routine. I felt that I wasn't pulling my weight—that I was a fifth wheel. Besides, I wanted a few silver dollars in my pocket. When I told wise old Nicolai, the head of my adopted family, that I wanted to go trapping, he understood. He loaned me a few dozen traps, a Yukon sled, snowshoes, an ax and an enormous Kodiak bear skin that must have squared ten feet. The bear skin was invaluable. It served me well as a tent, windbreak, and sleeping bag. Rolled up in the great skin, I was warm and comfortable on the coldest nights. For grub I had a few pounds of rice and beans in addition to plenty of smoked salmon which I also used for bait. Before leaving, Nick showed me how to make figure-four deadfalls and how to make sets for foxes in deep snow. When I mentioned that I would share whatever fur I took with him he seemed pained. I don't suppose it occurred to him that I would do otherwise. After all I was a member of the family, wasn't I?

Early one morning I mushed up the river, pulling my sled until I reached Afognak Lake, a body of water six miles long that nearly bisects the island. For a week I labored hard setting traps and deadfalls on both shores of the frozen lake. I had no permanent camp but simply spread my bearskin in any grove of trees I happened to be near when it became too dark to travel. With all my traps and deadfalls operational, I settled into a disciplined routine. Regardless of weather, from dawn until dark I tended my trapline along the shores of the lake and up tributary creeks. The results were disappointing. It was a bad winter, the snow piled up deeper and deeper and there were a couple of severe cold snaps. One night late in February it grew so cold that I could hear the spruce trees popping like rifle shots. Some days I took no fur at all but I kept plugging away, doing the best I knew how and running my traps whether I wanted to or not.

One day in mid-March, I spread my bearskin under a tall spruce tree, built up a big fire and took stock of my situation. The brutal weather, the incessant toil and monotonous diet were taking their toll. I was having trouble with my eyes. On bright days the reflection of the sun on the snow blurred my vision and at times it felt as though there was sand under my eyelids. My legs were becoming weak and I would stumble. My supply of beans and rice was exhausted and I was subsisting on a straight diet of smoked salmon. I had no reserve of fat on my body to give me energy. I was starving. Unless I wanted to become a statistic, it was time to pick up my traps, spring my deadfalls, take what fur I had, and return to the village, where I could get food, shelter, warmth, and rest. However, before making my final pickup, I decided to investigate a small stream that flowed in a general westerly direction toward a bay on the far side of the island from where the great mountains of the mainland were clearly visible. I suppose that I had traveled no more than half a mile down the creek when I came onto a blaze chopped on a spruce tree.

I was curious. All that winter I had seen no sign of another man. This blaze was the first indication that another trapper was in the area. I continued downstream until I came to another blaze, then another and another. Had I been thinking logically I would have turned back, but I continued down the little valley. Finally I came to a trap that held a dead, frozen otter. In its death struggles the animal had beaten down a wide semicircle in the snow the length of the trap chain that was fastened to a tree. Because I was weary I sat on a fallen tree and surveyed the scene as I rested. There were no tracks in the snow. Whoever had set that trap hadn't visited it for a long while—perhaps for two weeks or more. I couldn't believe that a professional trapper would leave a trap unattended that long. Maybe the man had left the country. Perhaps he had died. I considered these things as I examined the otter. It was a fine animal with a pelt that would bring seven or eight dollars properly skinned and handled. I removed the frozen carcass of the animal from the trap, placed it atop the sled and started back toward the lake. Because of my great weakness it took me a long while to retrace my steps. At the upper end of the lake I made camp in the shelter of the spruce trees. Here I rested the remainder of the day and all that night, forcing myself to eat the smoked fish that nauseated me, and sleeping fitfully. I melted snow in my cooking pot and drank the warm water which seemed to alleviate the cramps in my stomach and warm my whole body.

Two days later I had all my traps and gear loaded on the sled and was ready to start mushing toward the village a long ten miles away. As I came out of the forest onto the frozen lake it was pure chance that I happened to glance to my left. There a half mile distant was a man following the trail I had made when I returned from the valley with the frozen otter. I pulled the sled back into the woods, picked up my rifle, jacked a shell into the chamber, took up a position behind a tree and waited. Obviously I was being stalked by the man from whom I had stolen the fur. By the time he had covered half the distance separating us I could see that he was traveling on snowshoes and carrying a rifle. As he approached closer it was apparent that he was a bearded white man, a stranger, certainly no one from the village, and traveling very determinedly and rapidly in my direction. When he was about fifty yards away I rested my rifle over a spruce limb, aimed carefully about a foot above his head and squeezed the trigger. At the crack of the rifle the man stopped a moment, then moving very fast for a man on snowshoes, made for the woods. Again I fired, aiming this time a few feet ahead of the man. I must not have had a very good hold because the bullet splattered the snow in front of the man much closer than I intended. He stopped moving, threw up his arms in a gesture of surrender, and began moving directly away from me. Again I fired high over his head. Once more he threw up both hands and began running—a very difficult thing to do wearing snowshoes. When my visitor finally disappeared from sight I once more began the long, slow trek toward the village. Long after dark I arrived there near complete exhaustion. I could not have traveled much farther.

A year or so later I was in Kodiak. I went into Ben Kraft's store to buy supplies. There standing at the counter was the man who had stalked me the previous winter. Our eyes met. I knew him but he didn't know me. For that I am thankful!

Wilderness trapping can be exciting, frustrating, exhausting, and sometimes good for the body and soul. It may even be profitable. But it's not a sport like hunting squirrels or jigging codfish.

Hasselborg the Hermit

Mole Harbor is situated on the east side of Admiralty Island. From the mouth of the bay one can see the mighty mountains and the glaciers on the mainland. Looking toward the west can be seen the rolling hills and mountains of what must be one of the most beautiful landscapes on earth. The bay is shaped somewhat like the clenched fist of a left-handed man, with the index finger extended and pointing toward the heart of the island. At the tip of the finger, where the river enters the bay, was the cabin where Allen Hasselborg lived alone for more than fifty years.

Hasselborg was my friend. I became acquainted with him in 1947 and frequently visited with him until his death in 1954. He was a famous bear hunter, guide, philosopher, and recluse. Wise in the ways of men, sage in the lore of the wilderness, he was truly one of the greatest men of his time and certainly the most remarkable human being I have ever known. There will never be another man like him and the world is the poorer for that.

In the fall of 1949 I formed a trapping partnership with a long, lean, satunine man named Frank. Frank was broke. So was I. But Frank had a boat, and I had sixteen dozen traps. That's how it

113

came about that we dropped our anchor in the lee of the north shore of Mole Harbor one rainy day in November. We needed meat so I went ashore in the dinghy to shoot a deer. The rifle I carried was a .218 Bee with a 4X telescopic sight. Although this rifle had been designed for varmint shooting, in the hands of an expert marksman it was adequate for the small southeastern Alaska deer.

I intended to hunt the muskegs that lay parallel to the beach and extended back to the hills. To reach the open muskegs I had to cross a fringe of heavy timber about one hundred yards wide where the underbrush was extremely thick. I crossed through this cover without incident. When I reached the open muskeg, I loaded my rifle and started hunting. I soon realized that the chance of getting a deer that evening wasn't good. The wind was tricky and sign was poor. However, I decided to be patient, hunt the day out and see what happened. When the light began to fade and I had seen no deer, I reentered the timber that lay between me and the beach. Here the gloom of approaching night deepened and I hurried to get through before complete darkness.

I hadn't traveled more than a hundred feet when I heard a sound that stopped me dead in my tracks and caused the short hairs on the back of my neck to rise. It was an ominous, chilling, moaning growl. It was a sound I had heard before. I was sure that directly ahead of me in the thick brush there was a wounded grizzly bear that might attack at any moment. There have been few times in my career that I have felt as lonely as I did that evening alone in the gloom of the dripping rain forest with a wounded bear a few feet away that I could hear but not see. Slowly I backed away until I reached the muskeg. Here, I sat down to think things over. It was highly unlikely that the beast would come out of the woods to attack in the open. That just isn't the way grizzlies operate. It was getting darker by the minute. I had to do something and do it quickly. I could either go through the woods and take my chances with the bear, or I could spend a miserable night on the muskeg, nursing along a sickly fire of wet hemlock in the rain.

Damning people who left wounded bears in the woods and figuratively kicking myself for not bringing along my .375 Magnum rifle instead of wandering about in grizzly bear country with a peashooter, I reentered the woods. This time, however, I walked down about one hundred yards before leaving the muskeg. Then I checked my flashlight. The batteries were fresh and the beam strong. Flashing the light ahead and making plenty of noise, I went through the woods that bordered the beach without incident.

It was good to be out of those woods. What had started as a routine afternoon hunt for deer might well have had a tragic finale. I was lucky. I was thinking these thoughts and waiting for the adrenal fluids in my system to subside and the rapid beating of my heart to slow, when I saw a man emerge from the woods a few hundred feet away. He was heavily bearded, walked with an inimitable style, and carried no rifle. It was Allen Hasselborg.

"So it's you!" he said, when he caught up with me.

I admitted that it was indeed me.

"What were you doing back in those woods?" he demanded.

I said that I had been hunting deer.

"There aren't any deer back there," said the old man. "They're all over on the other side of the bay. You should have come up and talked to me first. I'd have told you where to hunt."

"Wish I had!" I said. "By the way, there's a wounded brownie back in the woods. Who's been in here hunting lately?"

Hasselborg looked at me keenly. "How do you know there's a wounded bear in these woods?"

"Because I heard it, several times, just a few minutes ago. Unless that bear has moved it's not more than two hundred yards from us right now!" I answered.

"You're sure it was a wounded bear you heard?" he asked.

"Of course, I'm sure," I said. "Don't you suppose I know what a wounded bear sounds like?"

"Well, that wasn't no wounded bear you heard back there," the old man said. "That was me."

I could scarcely believe what I heard. The growling and moaning couldn't have been more realistic had it been made by a bear. It was the first time I had heard Allen Hasselborg talk like a grizzly bear. Later I would hear him talk *to* the bears and the bears talk *to* him. Then he went on to explain why he had gone back in those woods and made like a wounded bear. Lately, he said, the government people from Juneau had been coming to this area to hunt deer. He didn't like people, especially bureaucrats, to hunt near his cabin. Consequently, whenever a party would show up, the old man would enter the woods and make like a wounded bear. The procedure worked. Every last one of the visitors would leave the area rapidly. One chap ran out from under his hat and didn't stop to pick it up.

"If I'd have known it was you hunting in there, I wouldn't have wasted all that energy," Hasselborg said. "I thought it was another one of those government people."

I suppose that I knew Allen Hasselborg as well as anyone else in Alaska did. Although he was decidedly unsocial, rather than anti-social, I liked him and he seemed to like me. I shared his frugal fare with him many times and on occasion slept overnight at his cabin. Together we sat at the door of his dwelling and watched grizzly bears fish for salmon in the river one hundred feet away. These animals, the most fearsome carnivora on the continent and perhaps the most dangerous big-game animals on earth, paid us no attention. "They know me," was the way the old man put it. "Let a stranger come within half a mile of here and the bears disappear until he leaves. All except you. They're getting so they know you, too." I considered the remark a great compliment.

One night I was awakened from a sound sleep by a rattling of the cabin. Assuming it was just another mild earthquake, which are common in Alaska, I paid the event little attention and promptly fell asleep again. The next morning I asked Hasselborg if he had noticed the quake.

"Earthquake?" he asked. "That was no earthquake. That was a bear rubbing itself on the cabin! They do it all the time. One stuck its head in the window once and looked me right in the face. I could have tweaked its whiskers."

Hasselborg had an aversion to civilization, bureaucrats, and women. That may be why he came to Admiralty Island in 1904, as remote from his aversions as possible, built a cabin and lived there for fifty years. He had disciplined his life down to the simplest dimensions. Compared to Hasselborg, Thoreau was almost a piker. He was practically self-sufficient. Once he told me that his total annual budget for all expenses was forty dollars.

"All I have to do," he said, "is catch two mink or one beaver a year. I can do that in one day. That gives me the rest of the year to do as I please. And that's what I do, too—as I please."

Hasselborg had a wonderful and productive garden. Everything was organically grown. He used a fish and wild-hay compost with sea kelp added for fertilizer. Southeastern Alaska is not farming country but the old man harvested excellent beets, potatoes, carrots, parsnips, peas, cabbage, and even asparagus. He had strawberries, raspberries, and red currants in profusion. In the watershed of Mole River were enough wild berries to feed all the people living in Alaska. There were clams and mussels on the beach. In the bay were red snappers, halibut, sole, and cod. In the river were trout and salmon in wondrous numbers. The woods were full of deer. All this abundance of fish and game was free and to be had for the taking.

Hasselborg's cabin was a model of efficiency. It had one room with an attic upstairs and an adjacent lean-to that served as workshop and storage area. The main room, which was about 16x12, served as kitchen, dining room, library and armory. The attic was the bedroom where Hasselborg slept on an enormous bear rug that must have measured ten feet square.

As one entered the downstairs room, the corner to the right was the kitchen. Here was the stove, frying pan, dish pan, bread pans, table, two chairs, and culinary equipment for two persons. Directly adjacent and two steps from the stove was the sitting room with a window facing the river. The corner to the right was the library. Here, neatly placed on shelves, were exactly eighty-seven volumes. There were books on the subjects of nature, hunting, travel, history, and many of the classics, including the complete works of Shakespeare. I doubt that Hasselborg had much formal education, but he certainly was one of the most literate men I have known.

My friend owned two boats. One was a canoe hand-hewn from a single spruce log. The other was a conventional wooden skiff about thirteen feet long. He used this, powered by an outboard motor, to make his annual trips to Juneau for supplies. I'm not sure that he went to Juneau each year. I do know that he frequently stated he would never go again. The combination of civilization, bureaucracy, and women was almost more than he could stand even for one day a year!

I don't mean to imply that Hasselborg abhorred women as such. Rather he considered them a nuisance, an unnecessary luxury. He preferred to live his life without them. When in their company, he was a complete gentleman. Once I brought the wife of one of my clients, and my own wife to Mole River to meet him. The old man treated them with extreme courtesy and respect. Each of these ladies was impressed and even charmed by this strange man who preferred the company of grizzly bears, eagles, otters and salmon to that of human beings—particularly females.

One summer while I was on Admiralty Island living with the bears, observing their behavior, sleeping on the ground, living on the bounty of the land and as remote from the electrified hysteria of civilization as is possible, I decided to visit Hasselborg. When I came up the trail toward his cabin I found the old man working in his garden.

"I knew someone was coming twenty minutes ago," my friend said. "I got plenty of watchdogs here—bears, geese, and eagles. They tell me when any strangers are around. I don't have to feed 'em or clean up after them, either!"

After supper that evening we sat on the doorstep of the toolshed overlooking the river and tidal flats. Salmon on the way to the spawning grounds up the river were splashing in the shallows. At the approach of twilight, Canada geese and mallards flew in and settled down for the night, all the while making sweet music. Eagles perched in tall trees making mouselike squeaking calls that sounded ridiculous coming from such an impressive and fierce-appearing creature. In the background and up the river a single lofty mountain dominates the region. That evening bathed in the rays of the setting sun, the mountain looked particularly beautiful.

"When I was hunting for hides I took many a fine bear off that mountain," said my companion. "Nobody hunts up in the high country anymore. There hasn't been a shot fired on that mountain for thirty-five years."

For a long while the old man seemed lost in reverie.

"I'd like to go back up there once more and just look around," he finally said. "I'd better do it pretty soon if I'm going to do it at all. I'm starting to get old." He continued to look at the mountain. "I saw an albino deer once in that big meadow you can see just below the snowline."

After our breakfast the next morning, Hasselborg remarked, "It looks like we're in for a spell of good weather. How would you like to make a trip with me back into the interior? We'll be gone a week or ten days or as long as we please. I'll show you some things that maybe you ain't never seen before."

Two hours later we started up Mole River. We each had a pack containing the barest essentials. I had my sleeping bag and an extra pair of socks. My companion had one blanket, and a short-handled double-bitted ax in a sheath. Each of us carried plenty of matches. As we traveled upstream, the old man led the

119

way, using a machete to clear brush when necessary. I carried my .375 Magnum rifle, fully loaded and with a few extra shells in my pocket. We had no grub. We were going to live off the country.

It was wonderful to watch Hasselborg travel in the woods and along the slippery gravel of the river bed. He seemed to glide rather than walk. Once he told me that he had never fallen down, and I believe it. Although at the time he must have been more than seventy years old, he seemed almost tireless. When we did stop for a brief rest on that day's journey up a wild river and through the virgin rain forest, the old man had the knack of relaxing completely, as a wild animal does. Though our resting periods were only of about ten minutes duration, Hasselborg would close his eyes and actually manage to nap a few minutes. When he awakened, he reminded me of a grizzly bear that has been suddenly disturbed when bedded down—instantly alert and loaded with energy.

The salmonberries and blueberries that grow so profusely on Admiralty Island were beginning to ripen. As we traveled we ate these berries. My friend stripped the fruit from the bushes and ate leaves, stems, hulls, and berries. Whatever went into his mouth he chewed and swallowed.

"If you're ever going to become a bear hunter," he said, "you've got to eat like a bear and live like a bear. Then maybe someday you'll start to think like a bear. If you're ever going to get any of these big, old wise bears that live back here in the mountain country, you have to think like a bear, act like a bear, and be at least as smart as a bear. Those government people from Juneau who come out here to hunt don't know anything about hunting bears. All they ever get are little scrubby orphans that even the bears won't associate with."

That evening we reached the headwaters of Mole River and entered an area of marshy meadows and small ponds. We bedded down in a small grove of yellow cedars near an abandoned beaver pond. The pond was full of small, undernourished, big-headed cutthroat trout. Hasselborg rigged up a pole with hook and line attached and, using a piece of red yarn for bait, began catching trout. Thirty minutes later we had a couple of dozen of these small trout spitted whole like a kabob broiling over our campfire. "Berries and fish," said the old man, "that's what the bears eat. No one ever seen an anemic bear or heard of one having a heart attack."

During the next several days we wandered about a wonderland of meadows, ponds, sub-alpine forests and grand vistas. We lived as our Cro-Magnon ancestors must have lived. We were hunters and gatherers. We were as free as it's possible for men to be in the twentieth century. We saw hundreds of deer and scores of grizzly bears. There were blue grouse, ptarmigan, beavers, mink, marten. Ducks raised their broods on the ponds, and twice we saw those most elegant of God's creatures— trumpeter swans. One day I shot a young beaver and our diet of fish and berries was varied by the addition of beaver tail, liver and haunch of beaver.

Some evenings as we rested by our campfire, Hasselborg would reminisce about the early days at the turn of the century when he hunted the great grizzly bears on Admiralty Island for their hides.

"There's sixteen hundred square miles on this island and I've hiked over and hunted on every one of those square miles," he said. "I knew every bear on some of these watersheds. And every one of those bears knew me, too. We got along fine together so long as we left each other alone. But when I hunted the bears, sometimes they would resent it and fight back. Yes, quite a few of 'em fought back! When they was able to. I've faced maybe twenty life-or-death charges in those days. One came awful close to getting me."

My friend took off his long-sleeved undershirt. His right arm at the elbow looked as though a heavy spike had been drilled into the muscle and then ripped out sideways. "Just one bite, that's all he got, but even so he pretty near bit off the whole arm.

121

It happened early one spring about forty years ago. The bear was hard hit with my .405 Winchester and died before he could finish me off." The old bear hunter put on his shirt and then continued. "I had a hard time of it the next few days. The snow was deep that spring. Took me three days to get down from the mountains to the beach and the arm swelled up pretty bad and began hurting. Then when I finally got down to the beach where my boat was I had a hell of a time getting the anchor up. You ever try to pull up a fifty pound anchor and chain in six fathoms of water with one arm? It ain't easy! Then after I got the anchor in I still had to hand crank the engine and steer the boat all the way to Juneau to see a doctor. I pretty near didn't make it."

"How did all this happen?" I asked. "Why did the bear charge?"

"How did all that happen? Why did the bear charge? I'll tell you why. Because I made a mistake! Now I've done enough talking for one day. I'm going to sleep."

So long as I live I shall never forget those glorious weeks I spent with Allen Hasselborg roaming the muskegs, meadows, and mountains of Admiralty Island's interior. For days on end we hiked through virgin, primitive wilderness. We drank sweet water from a hundred creeks; we breathed pure air into our lungs; we lived on the bounty of the land; we never saw the sign of another human being. Twice I saw the old man take grouse from the limb of a tree, hold them in his hands and croon to each one. The birds were absolutely trustful and made no effort to escape. "They think I'm God," he remarked. Once a young male grizzly that we encountered at close range unexpectedly became belligerent and demonstrated in a threatening manner. I covered the bear with my rifle in case it attacked, but my friend advanced slowly toward the beast all the while talking bear language. The animal quieted down and walked toward a patch of timber. Then, before the bear disappeared he snorted once and snapped his jaws ominously. "They're like a lot of people I've met," said Hasselborg. "They like to have the last word."

I would have been happy to have stayed up there the rest of the summer but one morning my companion said that his garden needed tending and that it was time to return to the cabin at Mole Harbor. Before leaving we took our last look at the glorious vista of the endless wilderness that lay stretched to infinity. "Three billion people on this earth and not a dozen will ever see what we're looking at!" Hasselborg said.

Two days later I said farewell to my friend and returned to town to attend to my affairs. I never saw Allen Hasselborg again. A short while later he entered the Pioneer's Home at Sitka and there he died. He lies buried in the cemetery overlooking Sitka Sound and the pulp mill that spews its poisonous fumes into the once pure atmosphere. I was told that pallbearers were hired for the internment. No publication in Alaska or anywhere else that I know of, mentioned by even a paragraph, the passing of one of the most remarkable men of the century. Several years later I was in Sitka in the winter but there was snow on the ground and I couldn't find his grave. I couldn't find anyone who knew where he was buried or, for that matter, was even interested.

Fishin' Fools

One summer I booked a party of four men from Tennessee for a six-day fishing trip. They arrived well-equipped with the finest of rods, reels, lines, leaders and miscellaneous paraphernalia, some of which I had not previously known existed. They even had landing nets—one for each man and two spares. I had heard of landing nets and had even seen pictures of them, but this was the first time I had seen them used for trout fishing in Alaska. *Landing nets!* Heavens to Betsy, what was Alaska coming to, I thought.

The first day of the expedition I took the men to an unnamed creek on the mainland, not far from our starting point of Petersburg. It really wasn't much of a trout stream by southeastern Alaska standards, but it was handy and I figured it was a good place to start. I will never forget those four dudes lined up on the bank of the stream making ready to assault the unsuspecting trout of this nameless stream in the wilderness of southeastern Alaska. Dressed in spanking new trousers, shirts, fishing jackets, waders and floppy brimmed hats into which were hooked all manner of lures flies and spinners, they were an imposing spectacle. I regretted that I hadn't brought along my camera to capture the scene for posterity.

I don't know how many trout these people caught that day using barbless hooks on a variety of lures. One hundred at least and perhaps twice that many. At the end of the day my clients were weary, happy, and in full agreement that they had never experienced such trout fishing. And all this on an unimportant creek that I called second rate at best!

I told these people that there were scores and hundreds of better creeks in Alaska and that in the course of our trip we would visit a few of them. Which we did. At the completion of this expedition my clients paid me off in full and added a handsome gratuity. They also presented me with six landing nets in practically mint condition. I hung these on the wall of the little room upstairs in our house in town which I used as an office. As far as I know, they are hanging there to this day. When I fished for trout in Alaska I was always happy to have a trout shake loose. It saved me the bother of unhooking it.

In some ways I enjoyed those summer fishing trips even more than the spring and fall bear hunts. Hunting grizzly bears was serious business. It was stressful. Sometimes it was disappointing. Not all of my clients got as large a bear as they had hoped to get. One of them didn't get any bear at all. Sometimes I was blamed when things didn't go according to plan. But I never guided a fisherman during my career who wasn't delighted with the salmon and trout fishing I showed him.

One of my favorite streams was Kadake Creek on Kuiu Island. Before the loggers came to clear-cut the watersheds to supply the pulp mills, this must have been one of the most beautiful watersheds anywhere. And such fishing! It was unbelievable.

I took the late Warren Page up Kadake Creek for a day's fishing when we were hunting black bears in the area in June 1949. Page was nearly as skillful with a rod and reel as with rifle and shotgun. Also he was a very precise fellow, and on this particular day he kept score. Each time he caught a trout he marked it down in a notebook. After six hours of fishing, he had taken three hundred and twenty-seven cutthroat trout. They

126

ranged from one to four pounds. The largest was twenty-five inches long and the smallest eleven inches. Though he used practically every lure in his tackle box, he had averaged slightly more than one trout for every two casts. We kept two fish for dinner that evening and released the rest.

Unlike most southeastern Alaska streams, Kadake is a gentle, almost placid creek. Its source is far back in the interior of the island where there are scores of cold springs and a maze of beaver dams. It flowed serenely from one deep pool to another through a magnificent forest of centuries-old spruce and hemlock trees. In May and June these pools were dark with cutthroat trout. Later when the salmon started to run, vast numbers of Dolly Varden trout followed the salmon upstream. These were pink and chum salmon not highly regarded as sport fish, but anywhere else except Alaska they would be considered superior game fish. Old-time Alaskans held the Dolly Varden trout in something akin to contempt. And I don't know why. Believe it or not, at one time there was a bounty on these trout. Trout tails in parts of Alaska were legal tender— twenty tails for a dollar! Moonshine whiskey was considered a bargain at two hundred trout tails for a gallon. It's difficult to understand the prejudice against the Dolly Varden. This fish is so similar to the Eastern brook trout that is native to New England that it takes an expert to distinguish one from the other. Yet I have heard Alaskans refer to these beautiful game fish as "sewer trout" and watched them toss Dollies they had caught back into the brush to die and rot because "there were too many of them in the creek." Undoubtedly these people were lineal descendants of those who believed there were too many passenger pigeons in Pennsylvania and too many grizzly bears in California!

During August and September many thousands of coho salmon fresh from the cold water of the blue Pacific Ocean came into Kadake Creek to spawn. Blue-backed, silver-sided, streamlined, strong and handsome, this fish has no peer as a fighter in Alaska or perhaps anywhere else. Pound for pound, it may be the most spectacular and exciting fish that swims. It takes a highly skilled fisherman to land a ten-pound coho on six-pound test line. The savage strike of this silver-hued warrior is a dramatic experience. Once hooked, the coho leaps, makes swift runs, dodges, twists, seeks shelter under log jams, and frequently races downstream until all the line on one's reel is exhausted and breaks. I always advised my clients to bring along plenty of spare line when fishing for coho salmon. Very probably it would be needed.

Kadake Creek! What a paradise it was! I remember the long, still reaches bordered by tall spruces that were ancient when the first explorers came to Alaska. And I remember the deep pools that were dark with resting trout and salmon. Everywhere there was wildlife. Feeding trout dimpled the pools, salmon spawned in the rifles, bald eagles soared high in the sky or perched in the trees. There were beavers and otters and bears. Always there were black bears—summer and fall. It was a poor day when we didn't see half a dozen or more blackies when hunting or fishing Kadake Creek.

One memorable day I shall never forget, however long I live, was the time were serenaded by timber wolves. Three of us were fishing for cutthroat trout using dry flies when suddenly the wolves began howling back in the muskeg a quarter mile away. We reeled in our lines and listened. No music on earth is as thrilling or as sad and moving as the howl of timber wolves. It was beautiful. As the glorious music echoed against the hills all the creatures of the wilderness grew silent and listened. Where else but on Kadake Creek could such a thing happen?

There were other creeks, many others, in southeastern Alaska where the fishing was comparable to Kadake creek. At the moment I am thinking of one on the south side of Admiralty Island. Upstream about one mile there is a stretch of quiet water ten feet deep and two hundred yards in length. Here, during the summer and early fall, there were always several thousand trout lying in the clear, still water. There were so many you could scarcely see the white gravel of the creek bottom. I saw a man from Georgia catch thirty-seven trout in as many casts from this pool. Then he missed one! He sat down on the creek bank at the edge of the woods and murmured, "If I didn't see it, I wouldn't believe it."

The rest of the day he and his partner had a ball. As we moved up the creek they fished every likely looking spot and some not so likely appearing. There were big trout, everywhere there was water. They caught fish on flies, spoons, spinners, elderberries, bass poppers, and even on a plastic worm. Toward evening a fair-size grizzly came out of the woods upstream and stared at us contemptuously. My friends decided they didn't care to compete with this most impressive looking resident of the area. So we returned to camp taking with us priceless memories and two pink-meated, fat trout for our supper.

Another stream that I remember with fond nostalgia is situated on the south side of Baranof Island and flows into a bay of spectacular beauty. From the time the ice begins to go out in April until it starts to form again in October, the fishing here was just a bit better than superb. A few hundred feet from the mouth of this stream an ancient rock slide had dammed the creek, forming a deep lake two hundred yards long and half that wide. I wouldn't begin to estimate how many trout and salmon congregated here before ascending to the main lake, which was the source of the stream.

In May 1940, when I was commercially fishing for trout, my partner and I caught five thousand pounds of Dolly Vardens from this pond in a few days. We could have taken ten times that amount, but both our time and the market was limited.

There used to be an annual run of about thirty thousand sockeye salmon in this stream. They came early in June and continued to run into July. This salmon is the darling of cannerymen because of its rich firm red meat that retains its texture and color even when cooked an hour at high heat. The

129

sockeye salmon is primarily a plankton feeder. It used to be assumed that it was purely accidental when one took any kind of a lure or bait. However, some lures attract these fish. Once in the course of a late spring bear hunt my two hunters and I came into a bay where there was a tremendous showing of sockeye salmon. Several hundred were gathering at the mouth of a creek and engaging in aerial acrobatics. It was too early in the day to start hunting bears, so more to put in the time than anything else, I took my clients in the skiff with their sport fishing gear and rowed into the midst of the school of salmon. The men started casting with a variety of spinners, spoons flies and wobblers but not one fish showed the least interest. Then one of the men tied on a lure that looked somewhat like a cross between an undernourished mouse and a Chinese blow fly. When he cast this monstrosity onto the surface among the leaping salmon, Whammo! Bingo! An eight-pound male sockeye mouthed it like it was manna from fish heaven. Immediately his partner emptied the tackle box looking for a similar lure. There was none. So the two men took turns using that the rest of the afternoon. They caught many salmon and enjoyed fine sport. Although I have never seen another lure as successful for catching sockeye salmon, I have heard that there are certain flies that will take these elegant fish.

Hunting grizzly bear and fishing for trout or salmon on the same creek at the same time are not compatible pursuits. You do one or you do the other—you don't do both. When you walk up a salmon stream in southeastern Alaska where there are grizzlies, you will almost certainly see one or two or more bears in the course of a day's journey. If you walk up enough creeks, over a long enough period of time, you will surely one day meet a bear that resents your intrusion. Such a bear may attack. And if and when a grizzly does attack, the traveler had better be ready with his rifle and not be encumbered with a fishing rod or any other unnecessary paraphernalia. This is something that is not even debatable. But not all of my clients believed this when I told them.

One September day I took a client up a creek on Baranof Island to hunt grizzly bears. I had explained to this chap that it was unwise to attempt to hunt bears and fish for salmon simultaneously. Evidently he decided that I didn't know what I was talking about because as we started up the creek he carried his rifle in one hand and his fishing rod in the other. When we reached the head of a pond and he saw thousands of coho salmon practically begging to be caught, he lost all sense of perspective. He forgot that he had traveled thousands of miles and expended thousands of dollars to hunt bears. He tossed his rifle to the ground as though it were contaminated and began casting for the salmon. My man was so engrossed with the showing of fish that he didn't notice the very considerable amount of bear sign that was evident everywhere. While my man was engaged in fishing operations I settled down to watch for any movements in the alders that surrounded us that would indicate that a grizzly was approaching to do a bit of salmon fishing itself!

In the next hour or so, my client hooked many salmon and even landed a couple. Then it happened. My companion had just hooked into a particularly wildly acrobatic fish when a grizzly bear suddenly came out of the alder brush no more than one hundred feet upstream and began moving toward us. I hollered to my friend to get his attention and at the same moment the bear reared up on its hind legs to get a better look. Reluctant to lose his valuable rod, the dude made a mighty lunge backward holding tightly to the rod. When the line parted he fell spread-eagled into the creek. When he regained his feet he tried to reach shore and lay hold of his rifle but went down into the water once more. All this outlandish activity was too much for the bear. It panicked! Leaping into the alders it took off in overdrive. Ten minutes later I spotted it far up the mountainside still going strong. That bear may have lived another twenty years, but I'll bet it never came back to that watershed. After that episode, my client agreed there was no way a man could hunt bears and fish at the same time. And he was right!

There are hundreds of lakes in Alaska that are so seldom fished that the trout die of old age. I know a few of these. At the moment I'm thinking of one that is accessible only to those with stout legs and leather lungs. Usually these remote, underfished lakes are full of stunted fish, but this particular one had rainbows that weighed five pounds. It was an unusual body of water. An old-timer told me that he sounded the lake once with a ball of twine one hundred fathoms in length but couldn't reach bottom.

Not only are there many seldom-fished lakes in southeastern Alaska, there are also many streams that don't know a sport fisherman for years on end. I happened on one years ago that I didn't know existed. Nor did many other people in Alaska know of it, either. It wasn't on any map of the area I have ever seen. But the summer that I happened upon it the creek was loaded with Dolly Varden trout that ran from three to seven pounds. I lived in Alaska nearly half a century but never before, nor since, have I seen such trout. And in a stream that probably had never had a lure or a fly cast upon its waters. I devoutly hope no one since has discovered this lovely watershed and decided to "develop" it.

The year that Alaska attained statehood, I took a party of six sportsmen from a midwestern state on a trout and salmon fishing expedition. Before they arrived I set up a camp along a clear, cold stream that was tributary to one of the main rivers on Admiralty Island. We had the entire watershed to ourselves— sixty square miles of virgin wilderness. This was our home for seven days, and our only neighbors were grizzlies, otters, deer, eagles, and waterfowl. We spent much of our time roaming through the cathedral-like forest, marveling at the beauty all around us. We caught huge halibut and tasty red snappers in the adjacent bay. We watched bears catch salmon and in the evening we relaxed around our campfire. We also did some fishing in the river. At the end of the trip we estimated that we had caught and released about fifteen hundred trout and three hundred salmon.

Where else on this continent is there such fishing? Nowhere! And I'll hang my hat on that!

Black Bear the Hard Way

Certainly the black bear is the easiest of all North America's big-game Carnivora to hunt. The animal is practically blind. It cannot distinguish a man standing motionless one hundred feet away. It has no protective coloration. Black stands out vividly against almost any background, be it green, brown, or white. A black bear's hearing is about as good as that of an average human, which is to say it's not very keen. When pursued by a yapping dog one tenth its size, a blackie will shinny up a tree and remain there until the dog leaves or a hunter comes along to shoot the bear. Where hunting pressure is minimal, black bears have a bad habit of bedding down out in the open—in a meadow, for example. Several times I have walked up onto sleeping bears and watched them awhile before finally slipping away without the bear's being aware of my presence.

Stalking a black bear is absurdly easy. All the hunter has to do after spotting the animal is walk toward it until within rifle range. I have done this many times across open ground with no protection whatever, much to the amazement of clients who had read stories relating to the difficulty of hunting black bears. I remember the time when I was guiding Lew Bulgrin and Jack

O'Connor on an Alaskan bear hunt. We spotted what appeared to be a dead blackie lying in a patch of sedge at least two hundred yards from the nearest cover. Lew and I went over to investigate while Jack stayed behind to watch the operation through his binoculars. Though we were hunting bears and Lew carried his rifle, we made no effort to approach the bear with caution. I suppose we were within fifty feet of the beast when I noticed it move.

"Lew," I said, "that bear's alive. You better shoot him."

"Wake him up, Ralph," Lew said. "It's against my principle to shoot a sleeping animal."

So I clapped my hands together and when the bear opened its eyes and looked at us stupidly, Lew killed it. Later Jack said he wouldn't have believed such an occurrence had he not witnessed it.

When I earned a livelihood guiding big-game hunters, black bears were unbelievably numerous along the mainland and on some of the adjacent islands of southeastern Alaska. There were hundreds of productive salmon streams where the bears congregated to grow sleek and heavy on the rich meat of the salmon that came in vast numbers to spawn in the summer and fall. There were innumerable meadows and tidal flats lush with vegetation and wild berries where bears that had never seen a man or heard a rifle shot came to feed. In those days before the loggers came to clear-cut the valleys, build roads, create massive erosion and destroy an irreplaceable wilderness, there were more bears than men.

Black bears were so plentiful, inoffensive and easy to hunt that early in my career as a guide I lost whatever respect I may have had for them previously. I just couldn't take them seriously. When guiding clients for blackies I didn't even carry a rifle. I considered it excess and unnecessary baggage. But there was one time on a black bear hunt that I most devoutly wished I had carried my rifle. Because I didn't, my reputation and career might have gone down the drain. Worse yet, I might have lost a client. That sequence of events might well have ended in tragedy.

In the late 1950s I booked a twenty-day fall bear hunt with a man from Uruguay. My client's prime objective was to shoot a trophy-size Alaskan brown bear. Then, if time permitted, he wanted a good representative black bear. I told this gentleman that getting a brownie might entail some hard work, a bit of luck and even a modicum of danger. However, I assured him that getting a black bear was like shooting fish in a rain barrel.

We started the hunt on Admiralty Island for brownies. Conditions were nearly perfect. There was a fair run of salmon that year, the creeks were low, and the weather was delightful. Day after day we prowled the salmon creeks, seeing bears every day. Conditions were so favorable and the brownies so numerous that we hunted very selectively. Almost too selectively, in fact, because time was becoming a factor when one day we came onto the bear we wanted in thick cover at very close range. I have never enjoyed these close encounters with Alaskan brownies, but because of the time factor I told my friend to shoot. He was a veteran of African and Asian big-game hunts and a cool chap. He killed the huge animal neatly and efficiently with a minimum of fuss. We had our trophy!

The next day I moved our floating camp to the mouth of Kadake Creek on Kuiu Island. This was one of my favorite black bear creeks and with two full days of hunting left I was completely confident that my client would get his black bear trophy without incident.

We were enjoying sourdough pancakes with maple syrup the next morning when it started to rain. By the time we were ashore and heading for the mouth of the creek it was raining harder and a brisk, fresh wind was blowing from the southeast. The fine weather was over and the fall monsoons had begun. Tough times lay ahead.

Kadake Creek drains an enormous watershed of ponds, lakes, muskegs, and tributary creeks. An inch of rain can mean a rise of two feet or more in the main stream. Ordinarily we should have seen half a dozen bears as we traveled up the first mile of the stream, but as a matter of fact we saw none. With the wind swirling erratically up the river spreading our scent, it would have been strange indeed if we did see a bear. However, I hoped to get up the creek closer to the headwaters where the large bears were more apt to be and hunt downstream later in the day when the wind would be in our favor.

With only a couple of hours of daylight left and the creek rising rapidly, I decided we had best start back. At that very moment we spotted a bear investigating a tributary stream. It was a fine trophy-size blackie and was facing away from us. We were lucky. We might have hunted a month and not seen a better bear. I nodded to my client, and he placed a 220-grain soft-nosed bullet into the animal's neck at the base of the skull. The bear was dead before it fell into the water.

In those days I could skin a bear—any bear—in about thirty minutes. I peeled the hide off this one in twenty minutes. Before starting the operation I honed my knife, then laid the stone down onto a gravel bar. When I finished there was an inch of water covering it. By the time I had removed the skull from the pelt and trimmed off some of the surplus fat, the water on the gravel bar was ankle deep. The rain had become a downpour, the wind was moaning ominously in the tall trees, and the river was reaching flood stage. Even as I surveyed the scene, a log thirty feet long and two feet in diameter came floating down the river. Such an object might easily crush or drown a man caught in midstream.

Ordinarily, getting a bear hide down a stream is no problem. One simply ties a line to a forepaw and floats it to tidewater where it can be picked up with a skiff. However, with the creek at flood stage as it was this day, such a procedure was not only difficult, it was hazardous. But standing there in a veritable cloudburst in a rapidly flooding creek would solve nothing, so I made a decision. First I tied a short piece of line to one of the bear's paws and the other end around my waist. Then I gave my hunter some instructions.

"Now listen carefully," I said. "We're about two miles from the beach. At the last bend of the creek just before tidewater there's a big dead snag. Now I'm going to float, drag and hassle this bear hide down to that snag. When I get there I'm going to build a fire—a hell of a big fire. You're going to be able to see that fire half a mile away even through all this rain. It's going to light up the woods like a burning house. But I can't build that fire until I get there and that's going to take some doing. I'm going to go right down the middle of the river and I'm going to get wet. Most of the time I'll be waist deep in water and sometimes I'll be up to my neck where I can drink standing up. I don't want you to go through all that misery. So I'm going to send you down through the woods. Just inside the timber you'll find a good bear trail. All you have to do is stay on that trail and keep slogging along until you come to a small creek where there are beaver ponds. You can either bull your way through these or make a wide circle to your left and bypass them. Once you're past the beaver ponds,you should see the glow of my fire and you're practically home free."

"Your fire!" he said doubtfully. "How can you start fire in such wetness of weather?"

"Don't you worry about that," I assured my client. "I'll have a fire long before you get there. A big fire. The biggest fire you've ever seen. I don't care how much it rains, I can always start a fire."

"Just like shooting fish in barrel," my sport said.

"That's right," I answered. "Just like shooting fish in a rain barrel!"

When I took my hunter into the woods, showed him the bear trail he was to follow and started him on his way, I was making a colossal error of judgment and the most serious breach of conduct a professional guide can commit. The first and cardinal rule of guiding big-game hunters is that the safety and welfare of the client shall be foremost and above all other considerations. Yet, here I was, leaving a client from a different continent who was totally unfamiliar with the terrain in a trackless wilderness in a howling storm with darkness approaching! But at the time I thought of none of these things. My concern was to get the bear hide down the creek before flooding became much worse. And as quickly as possible.

A freshly skinned bear hide is heavy. When it's soaking wet, it's much heavier. In some deep, flooding creek you don't really float or drag such a burden—it drags you. It was a wild trip down Kadake Creek. Several times I was swept off my feet and dragged over gravel bars and boulders and into deep pools where I went completely out of sight. Twice I was nearly sucked into log jams where I might easily have drowned. Through it all I hung onto the pelt until far ahead in the gathering gloom I spotted the big spruce snag on the hill above the final bend in the creek. Here I sat a few minutes—wet, chilled, bruised, weary, a bit scared, but extremely thankful to be alive and still in possession of the black bear hide.

I draped the hide over a log to drain before going up to the dead spruce to have a look. The tree was hollow and the wood inside dry as kindling wood stacked under a kitchen stove. I had plenty of matches, each one dipped in paraffin and carried in one of two waterproof containers. Plenty of spruce pitch, which burns better than kerosene, was available. Starting a fire was no problem. In a matter of minutes I had a fire roaring in the hollow trunk of the dead tree. The warmth and light cheered me immeasurably.

I stripped to my underwear and hung my boots and clothing on limbs to dry. By now the flames were climbing up the trunk of the snag. Soon the whole tree would be ablaze. Standing near the fire and absorbing that heat, I felt good. In fact I was extremely pleased with myself. In spite of the atrocious weather and attendant difficulties, I had got my client a superior trophy. There it lay draped over a log practically as secure as though it were in the pickling vat at the taxidermist's shop in Seattle. Any moment now my client would come striding out of the woods. Soon we would be back aboard our cruiser sipping hot toddies made of Hudson Bay rum, honey, and cinnamon.

Because of the heavy overcast and deluge of rain, darkness came early that evening. The roar of the flooding creek and the moaning of the wind were increasing. Time passed slowly. After an hour, I began wondering why my sport hadn't showed. The hardest part about waiting is waiting. There was nothing I could do. By now the snag was aflame clear to the top. The light surely could be seen from a distance of a thousand yards. For the first time that night I found myself wishing I had brought my rifle to signal my client. I was thinking along these lines when I heard, very faintly, a shot from a great distance up the river. I quickly moved back into the woods where it was quieter. Again I heard a shot, more distinctly this time. A few seconds later I heard a third shot.

Three slow shots—the sign of distress!

The recognized procedure was to fire an answering shot in return. My client was appealing for help and I couldn't answer. At that moment I believe I would have bartered my immortal soul for a rifle and a dozen cartridges. To return to the boat for my gun, leaving the fire where I had promised to meet my client, was wrong. To wander about through the trackless rain forest at night with no means of communication, on the improbable chance that I might locate my friend, was worse than stupid. I had no option but to wait, remain where I was, keep the fire blazing and continue to wait, and to wait, and to wait. And worry. My imagination began to run riot. I imagined my client far up the river lying helpless with perhaps (God forbid) a broken leg. Suppose he had stepped into a boghole and had drowned. The shots I had heard might have been fired in desperation just as he was sinking out of sight.

I castigated myself for having become separated from my hunter who had traveled thousands of miles to place himself in

141

my care. He had trusted me and I had betrayed his trust. How many times had I declaimed that a man must never venture into the wilderness without carrying certain essentials, including dry matches, flashlight, emergency rations, and a rifle with ammunition. All I had were matches—plenty of dry matches— enough to set half of Kuiu afire.

It must have been near midnight when I finally got hold of myself. Worrying and fretting would do no good. The situation was bad and there was no point making it worse. When daylight came I would go back up the river and find my friend if he were still alive. I would do whatever it was possible to do. Until daylight came I would remain by the fire, rest, sleep if possible, and conserve my strength.

I was making ready to arrange the bear hide as a kind of tent-like shelter where I could lie down and perhaps sleep when my missing hunter came out of the darkness of the forest into the light of the fire. He was a sight. His clothes were torn, he had lost his hat, his dark eyes staring from a white face looked like two holes burned in a blanket. And he was limping badly. He sat down heavily on a log without speaking. Obviously he was near total exhaustion. I was so happy I nearly embraced him.

I helped my friend undress and hung his clothing near the fire to dry. Then I examined him to find why he limped. His left ankle was rather badly sprained but except for innumerable scratches and bruises he was uninjured. After resting awhile my client put on his clothing and together we made our way through a fringe of timber to the beach where our skiff was secured. An hour later we were aboard our cruiser. Each of us was too exhausted to eat or even have a hot drink.

The next morning, taking advantage of the flooding tide I went to the mouth of the creek with the skiff and picked up the bear hide. The remainder of the day we rested aboard the boat, eating, sleeping, and thankful that the ordeal was over.

That evening as the cook prepared dinner, my client recounted the event of the previous day and night. He had traveled down the bear trail I had pointed out and had made good progress until he came to the beaver ponds. After looking over the maze of dams, canals, cuttings and pools of uncertain depth he decided to by-pass the area. He went back into the woods and with darkness approaching began what he thought was a wide circle to the left. In the gloom of the deep woods, in completely unfamiliar country and inexperienced in wilderness travel, he did a perfectly natural thing—he circled to the right. In a short while he became disoriented—which is to say—lost. It's no disgrace to be lost in the woods. Neither is it a calamity. The thing for the traveler to do when lost in the wilderness, especially at night, is to stop, build a fire, make himself as comfortable as possible and wait for daylight. But my friend had hired me to take care of such things, and I had deserted him.

So he did what many a man before him had done in such a situation: He continued to travel without knowing whether he was moving toward his destination or away from it. In the darkness he bumped into trees, got tangled in patches of devil thorns, stumbled, tripped over roots, and fell many times. Then his boot became entangled in a maze of roots and he fell heavily, spraining his ankle. Still he continued to travel until, finally, he came to the river. To his dismay he could see that he was walking *upstream*. Then, for no reason that he knew, he fired his rifle three times.

Firing the shots relieved his frustration and anxiety greatly. He knew where he was. All he had to do was walk down the river, never letting it out of sight or hearing until he again came to the beaver ponds. Then he would cross these even if he had to swim. Resolved to keep moving until he came to my fire or the beach, he began slowly and painfully retracing his journey downstream. By the time he reached the ponds he could smell smoke from the burning snag. Past the ponds he could see the glow of my fire. He'd made it.

It was as easy to shoot a black bear as it is to shoot a fish in a rainbarrel. I said it, but I know a man who doesn't believe it. He hunted only one day and killed a single bear, but on the basis of that brief experience I'm sure he considers hunting black bears much harder than shooting fish in a barrel!

When I Hire a Guide

If I become affluent enough before I hang up my rifles for the last time, I would like to hunt big game that I haven't hunted before in some land I have read about but never seen. I would like to hunt bighorn sheep in Alberta, where these animals that so many sportsmen rate as North America's number one trophy are the most plentiful and grow the largest horns. I think that I would like to hunt jaguars in the jungles of Central or South America. The world's great cats have always fascinated me, and I have been told that the jaguar is the hardest of all to find and stalk.

Then, of course, there is Africa. What big-game hunter worthy of the name hasn't dreamed of hunting in Africa. Ever since I was knee-high to a nanny goat I have dreamed of hunting there. Twice I have been invited to join an African safari and each time the arrangements fizzled out. But I may yet hunt in Africa, or what's left of it. If I go, I'll hunt mainly with a camera. I certainly have no wish to shoot an elephant, a rhino, or leopard. But a lion, yes! Provided that it could be taken in fair chase. A one-on-one proposition. One lion, one man. Both of us down on the ground and in the same patch of brush, with the beast having at least a mathematical chance of killing me before I kill it. I have never shot any animal over bait, and I'm not going to travel all the way to Africa to begin.

Ever since I began reading Colonel Jim Corbett's wonderful tales of hunting tigers in India, I have wanted to follow in his footsteps. Just being in the same block of jungle, timber or any other habitat with one of these sagacious, horrendous, almost mystical carnivores must be the supreme hunting adventure. Particularly so, if the tiger happens to be hunting you when you are hunting it! It's too much to suppose that I will ever meet a Bengal tiger in the jungles of India but one never knows. When I was a boy I used to dream of hunting the great bears of Alaska. I did hunt them, too—for more than thirty years.

Perhaps I won't hunt in any of the faraway places I dream of, but I'm going hunting somewhere once more before I go over the great divide. It may be only to Alabama for wild turkey or Wyoming for antelope. But wherever I go—South America, Wyoming, Alberta or Africa, Alabama or Asia—I'm going to need a guide, and I'm going to pick that guide with more care than most men do their wives. I know better than most men how great a factor the guide is to the success or failure of a big game hunt. All other things being equal, the guide is the catalyst of the hunting expedition. If the operation is successful, it will probably be due to the guide's expertise and dedication. If the hunt fails, you may be sure your guide is incompetent, lazy or just doesn't give a damn! I'm going to select my guide carefully—very carefully.

I had the great fortune to have known and worked with some of the outstanding guides during the golden age of bear hunting in Alaska. I hunted with Charley Madsen in 1933 when he was the only guide on Kodiak Island. I knew and hunted with Allen Hasselborg who lived with the great grizzly bears of Admiralty Island for fifty years and undoubtedly knew more about bears than any man of this century. When I was an outfitter-guide I worked with the legendary Hosea Sarber. Hosea was a strange

148

man. He semingly was utterly devoid of the natural emotion of fear. The more dangerous the situation, the greater the peril, the happier this man was. I have seen him deliberately crowd and antagonize bears, hoping they would attack. He was a superb rifleman in spite of being blind in one eye. I would say he was the best field shot with a rifle I have known. One day Sarber went into the woods on one of the islands of southeastern Alaska. It's the only time I knew him to travel in bear country without his rifle. He has never been seen since that day.

Another famous guide of that era was my old friend, Hardy Trefzger. I worked with Hardy in the Yakutat region on three glacier bear hunts as well as a couple of expeditions on Admiralty Island for grizzlies. He was a most remarkable man and I came to have a profound respect for him. Mount St. Elias is the third highest peak in North America. Before it was officially ascended by a well-equipped and financed party of moun- taineers in 1919, Hardy walked up the peak to its summit and back down again in *four* days! The only supplies he carried was a pocket full of raw oatmeal. Later in his career as a guide and while guiding a bear hunter, he was attacked by a female grizzly that thought her cub was being threatened. The bear mauled Hardy and in the fracas nearly bit his arm off and scalped him. The old frontiersman managed to make it back to his cabin without help. There he slapped the scalp back onto his head and treated his arm as best he could, using 151 proof Hudson Bay rum as an antiseptic. After this self-medication and first aid he drank what was left of the rum and went about his business.

I hope I can find a guide on this hunt I am planning like Trefzger or Hasselborg or Sarber. There may not be any such men living today but I'm going to keep looking and searching and hoping I'll find one.

I will avoid any guide who offers me a guaranteed hunt or who even promises that I will get shots at the game I seek. This is a sucker proposition for both guide and client. I know, because early in my career I used to advertise guaranteed Alaska bear hunts to prospective clients. I was very specific, too. *"No Bears, No Pay!"* I said, and signed my name. Looking back now, I wonder at my naiveté. However, I must say that it attracted a certain type of novice hunter.

I remember two chaps from Ohio who took me up on this proposition of no bears, no pay. They were rather blunt about it, too. When these people arrived in Alaska and even before we went through the usual formality of shaking hands, one said, "Young, if we don't get our bears, we ain't agoing to pay ya!" I didn't like what the guy said, nor the way he said it.

Two days later we were wading up a salmon stream on Kuiu Island when we came onto a female black bear and her two small cubs. Both cubs scrambled up adjacent trees. The sow evidently wasn't aware that female bears defend their cubs savagely and to the death as so many students of bear behavior insist they do, because she hastily and ingloriously fled into the brush, leaving her offspring to fend for themselves. So there we were, two brave hunters from southern Ohio and their faithful guide, in the Alaskan wilderness, looking up at trees where two spaniel-sized bear cubs clung to limbs thirty feet above, whining mournfully. "Well, well!" I said to one of the clients. "Look what we have here and so early in the trip. Two bears! Now, you shoot those bears—that's plural—bears, just like I guaranteed. Then we'll go farther up the creek and see if we can find some more bears for your friend to shoot."

"WAAAIT A MINUTE," he said. "Hold on now! Them's pretty small bears. Hell, I got a dog back home bigger than both them bears put together. I didn't come all the way to Alaska to shoot that size bears. I want *big* bears!"

"A bear is a bear," I said. "I guaranteed you would get bears. I didn't say anything about the size of the bears. You told me that if you didn't get bears you wouldn't pay me. I want to get paid. So go on, shoot the bears."

"I think we had better talk this over," he said. "So these two characters who had signed up for a guaranteed bear hunt, went into a huddle. In due time they decided they wanted to hunt for trophy-size bears and take their chances. After that, things went more smoothly. Although it was only a ten-day hunt, both of these novice hunters took representative blackies as well as a couple of grizzlies.

After that experience I never again guaranteed a client anything. I promised my hunters that I would do my best to make their trip pleasant and successful. I will be properly suspicious of any guide who promises to do more than that.

Before I close a deal with any outfitter-guide, I want to make certain that the man with whom I have contracted will be my guide on the hunt. By no means do I want to arrive in some faraway, strange land only to find that I have been "farmed out" to another guide, one whom I have probably never heard of. This very thing occurs all too frequently, and I don't want it to happen to me. I have heard some sad tales from hunters who have been farmed out. One chap told me that he hunted bears with a guide for ten weary days without seeing one of the animals. At the conclusion of the trip the guide admitted that he had never seen a wild bear in his whole life.

When I was in the business of guiding bear hunters, I invariably urged my clients to keep their party small. A group of two hunters was about right; three were acceptable. Sometimes under pressure I booked larger parties. Whenever this occurred, I made it a practice to hire licensed, registered guides as assistants. Most of these were excellent people, but a few were incompetent and even worse. One lad I hired held a valid license to guide big-game hunters in Alaska but didn't know how to skin a bear properly! Another got himself and the hunter he was supposed to be guiding lost, in an area where I didn't think it was possible to get lost. When I found these people two days later, they were briskly traveling along a bear trail in the wrong direction, and the faithful guide was in the lead! I'm going to look long and hard for an outstanding and reputable guide. When I find him, I want to hunt with him and no one else.

151

Surely I'll find the guide I want, and if I'm lucky we'll make a deal. Then it will be my responsibility to be as good a hunter as he is a guide. During my career as an Alaskan guide, it was my good furtune to have as clients some of the elite of the hunting fraternity. They were cooperative, understanding, agreeable and gave me the benefit of the doubt when I made mistakes—and I made plenty of them. When I did my job of finding game and putting them within reasonable shooting range, these hunters did the rest. All of these men were superb riflemen and made clean kills. Not one left me with the nasty and dangerous job of trailing a wounded grizzly in the southeastern Alaska jungle. I hope to conduct myself as these great hunters did. If I do, I know my guide will respect me as I did them. Every one of them!

I will try to accept the hardships, adversities, and imponderables that are incident to any wilderness hunt and do it cheerfully. Nothing is more distressing on a hunt than a crybaby who bemoans the weather, the perversity of the game being sought, the unavoidable malfunction of equipment, and even the lack of synthetic jam to spread on his pancakes. I don't know why such persons go hunting. They should stay home and breathe smog while eating things that go snap, crackle and pop!

While on the subject of cheerfully accepting the imponderables that are the warp and woof of big-game hunting, I think of an Eastern Airlines pilot who booked an October hunt, and right from the start nothing went according to plan.

I anchored our floating camp in a bay on the south shore of Admiralty Island. There were three salmon streams tributary to the watershed and ordinarily all of them were highly productive of salmon and bears. This season, however, the salmon run was below normal and the grizzlies weren't as plentiful as we expected. But we hunted hard, and although we saw a fair number of bears, we couldn't find the trophy-size animal we wanted. So one day, on a hunch, we left our camp and ran over to another bay a few miles away with my outboard-powered skiff, where I hoped we would find more favorable conditions and more bears. Late that afternoon we had hiked to the spring-fed source of the main stream. Here we settled down, concealing ourselves in the brush at the edge of the stream, to wait for the big old boar grizzly that would sooner or later show himself. The rain that had been intermittent since morning became a downpour. The wind that had been merely a stiff breeze became a gale. The watershed we were on was notorious for flooding and I knew we had to get back to our skiff while it was still possible. We crossed the creek and struck out for the muskeg and higher ground. Enroute to the beach we encountered two bears that were doing what we were—leaving the flooding stream and seeking higher ground. One of the bears was a fair-size trophy but we couldn't spare the time it would have taken to shoot it and skin out the pelt. It was a matter of life or death that we reach our skiff before it was swamped by the torrential rain or smashed to splinters by the gale-force wind.

It was nearly dark when we arrived at the beach, and we were thankful to find our skiff still afloat and undamaged. We bailed out our boat, started the motor, and bucked into the wild gale toward an abondoned Indian smokehouse half a mile away that I knew about. Here we sought shelter—two weary, bedraggled, cold, wet, hungry, disappointed bear hunters.

A southeastern Alaska smokehouse is just that—a structure specifically designed and built to smoke-cure salmon. Basically, it's a large square box with a hole in the roof to allow excess smoke to escape. Fresh salmon are split and hung over poles above the fire of alder wood which is built on the gravel floor. This particular smokehouse had been used many long years and the rough hewn planks used in the construction were exceedingly well impregnated with smoke, tar, enzymes and other various carcinogens. Countless salmon had been smoked here for decades and the oil that had dripped from the fish above had made the gravel floor slippery and richly odoriferous.

My client was a civilized man and used to the better things in life. But all that dark, long night lying on a bed of foul-smelling gravel in an Indian smokehouse while listening to the wind moaning and the fierce rain pelting the crude shelter, my friend uttered no word of complaint. Not once did he censure me for failing to bring along emergency rations in case of a misadventure such as ours. He didn't complain about being hungry. Neither did he ask me what I planned to do if the storm continued to rage for a week and we remained stranded on a tiny islet in a miserable smokehouse without sustenance. Instead, he seemed to be actually enjoying the experience.

All night I kept a fire smoldering with wood the Indians had stacked outside. When daylight finally came, each of us had turned a couple of shades darker and my guess is that we smelled similar to two sides of kippered salmon. Later in the day the storm moderated and we made it back to camp safely but with no bear trophy.

The remainder of the hunt was anticlimactic. Due to the flooding of the creeks the grizzlies couldn't fish for salmon and had moved back into the hills to feed on berries. Though we hunted hard we saw only an occasional traveling bear, all of them small. The upshot was that my sport went home without a trophy—skunked. He was the first man I had guided in my career who didn't get a bear.

When my pilot-client arrived back home he wrote to the Alaska Game Commission telling them of the wonderful bear hunting trip he had made that fall. He also extolled the capabilities and dedication of his guide, Ralph W. Young. Later I booked clients who had been referred to me by this same fine gentleman, or "Bearless Joe," as he liked to call himself.

When I go on that final hunt I am planning, I hope I conduct myself as this gentleman did on the bear hunt we made together long years ago on Admiralty Island in Alaska. If I do, I will have earned the honorable title of sportsman and gentleman.

Summer of the Trumpeter

Admiralty Island in 1961 was the "Summer of the Trumpeter Swans." Due to the cancellation of a trip, my spring bear hunting season had ended two weeks earlier than scheduled. It was early in June, the bear hides taken earlier had been shipped to the taxidermist in Seattle, my hunting equipment had been overhauled and stored ready for the fall guiding season, and idleness burdened my soul like the memory of a dark deed performed long ago. I might have painted my dwelling or mowed the brush on my property or even sought a paying job for the summer. However, none of these options appealed to me. Instead, I had a powerful desire to get back to the wilderness and away from the stress and harassments of civilization. For awhile, at least, I wanted to be where I didn't have to listen to people who talked endlessly about nothing.

Early one morning I left town aboard my diesel cruiser and headed northwest toward the beckoning white mountains of Admiralty Island where there were many grizzly bears and hardly any men. That evening I anchored in a snug cove on the east side of the island that few travelers knew existed. I went ashore and spread my sleeping bag under an ancient spruce.

Here I lay a long while, listening to the voices of the wilderness and the creatures that live there until I fell into a dreamless sleep that city dwellers never experience.

In the morning I hiked to a nearby creek where I hoped to find bears beginning to gather in anticipation of the annual run of salmon. A few fish were showing in the estuary but when I went upstream as far as the falls I saw none on the spawning beds or lying in the deep pools. Obviously there would be few grizzlies on the watershed for weeks.

For the next several days I loafed and enjoyed the sights and pleasures of that glorious, pristine wilderness. I ate clams that I dug at low tide and steamed over the coals of my campfires. I feasted on the salmonberries that were just beginning to ripen and I broiled red snappers and lemon soles that I caught near the kelp beds. I speared big, juicy Dungeness crabs in the shallows at the mouth of the creek. Sometimes I lay in the warm sunshine watching the bald eagles soaring high in the sky and I enjoyed the mink and otters that played along the shore. In the evenings deer came out of the woods to feed on the tender sedge that grew in the tidal zone. Once I saw a sow grizzly followed by two spaniel-size cubs walking the beach on the opposite shore. Life was so pleasing and easy that I felt almost guilty, though I don't know why.

I decided to take a trip into the interior of the island where I could observe the behavior of bears that lived away from the salmon creeks. I had always wondered how many bears lived in the high country as compared to those on the watersheds. So one delicious morning with the birds singing and every tree and bush sparkling in the sunlight, I left tidewater and started up the valley. I packed only my sleeping bag, spare clothing, a double-bitted ax, matches, knife, fishing gear and, of course, my .375 Magnum rifle and ammunition. With this outfit I could wax fat in the interior of the island until the snow came and much longer if necessary.

On my way up the valley I stopped to drink from a tiny rivulet that flowed into the main stream. At the base of a miniature falls there was a pool about twelve inches in diameter and perhaps ten inches deep. In this pool there was a fingerling coho salmon two and a half inches long. It was such a happy-appearing, bright fish that I sat awhile, watching it and speculating on its origin and destiny. While so engaged, a mosquito lit on my hand. As it prepared to sink its bill into my flesh, I gently squashed it with a finger. Then I picked up the quivering insect and dropped it on the surface of the pool. The little salmon rose swiftly, seized the insect, and sank back to the bottom. Seven times in the next hour I repeated the action and each time the little fish took the mosquito. I could see its belly becoming distended. When I dropped the eighth mosquito onto the pool, the fish rose slowly but with small enthusiasm. It took the insect into its mouth, held it a moment and spit it out. It had had enough to eat. I have known men who didn't know that much!

Late the same day I was back in the high country in the interior of the island, where few men had ventured. I finally came to a beaver dam that looked so inviting that I decided to camp there. It didn't take long to build a lean-to out of saplings and evergreen boughs. The structure was not an architectural triumph but it blended well with the background, it effectively shed rain, and it reflected heat. Basically, that is all any shelter will do. It was my home and refuge for nearly six weeks. I built it in two hours, and it cost nothing.

Like all beaver dams in that part of Alaska, this one swarmed with cutthroat trout. The fish population far exceeded the available food. As a result the fish were undersized, lean-bodied, white-meated, and hungry. That summer I caught hundreds of these trout using every lure imaginable. I caught fish with small spinners, hooks with a duck feather tied on the shank, hooks baited with red elderberries, a piece of yarn from a sock, and even with bare hooks. Had I stuck a finger in the pond I believe the trout would have attacked it. Each evening I would broil a dozen or so of these minnows over my fire, Indian fashion. Then I would eat them, heads, entrails, bones and all. If you are ever out in the woods for any considerable length of time and living entirely on the bounty of the land, I would advise you to do the same, if you want to remain well nourished and healthy. One reason you don't see any otters or seals in the wild that are anemic is that they eat the whole fish, not just the "choice" parts.

For several days I wandered happily in that glorious land abounding with wildlife, as free and self-reliant as the mountain men of the past century. Each day I saw blacktail deer, blue grouse, ptarmigan, and grizzlies. I saw one female bear with three cubs traveling up a mountainside. One cub was riding on her back like a jockey, successfully resisting its mother's half-hearted efforts to shake it loose. It was a priceless sight.

One evening while I was resting in my lean-to I heard the call of a trumpeter swan. The call of this bird has a ventriloquial quality so that I couldn't be sure how far away it originated or even from what precise direction it came. Twice more that evening I heard the call. The last time I was in my sleeping bag—half asleep, half-awake. I imagined I was listening to celestial music from heaven.

The next morning I hiked up a mountain to gain a few hundred feet elevation. From this vantage point I could see a pond that I didn't know existed. It seemed likely that the swan I had heard was resting on this pond. Two hours later I was there. It was an abandoned beaver lake. At the upper end I saw a trumpeter swan and four cygnets—her babies. For the remainder of the day I stayed close by the pond, utterly awed and fascinated watching these magnificent birds.

The gods of creation must have been in a generous and benign mood when they fashioned the glorious trumpeter swan. A pure white creature, except the feet and bill, it's the largest of the world's waterfowl. Although it weighs as much as forty pounds and has a wingspread of ten feet, it flies as swiftly and even more gracefully than a Canada goose. Swimming on a

160

wilderness lake, clean, noble and most elegant, it's pure living poetry. There must be a special place in hell for the person who would wantonly destroy one of these creatures. The call of the trumpeter is more reminiscent of a woodwind than a trumpet. It is unique among all the sounds in nature. Hearing it on a still evening in the wilderness of Alaska is a spiritual experience. Those people who teach that life began by chance and evolved according to precise mathematical formulae never heard the call of a trumpeter swan!

Each day of the several weeks that I lived in the high country that summer I spent a few hours with the swans. At first the birds were a bit nervous and even showed some resentment. Once when I approached the family a little too close, the old bird rushed toward me with neck outstretched and its wings beating furiously. It presented such a formidable appearance that I retreated up the bank. After seeing this demonstration, I have an idea that even a bald eagle or an otter would hesitate to attack one of these adult swans. In due time these charming creatures came to accept me as a part of the environment in the same way they tolerated the deer that came to feed along the shore and the mallard that was raising her brood of ducklings on the same pond. Once a cygnet swam toward me and, at a distance of about thirty feet, floated motionless, eyeing me speculatively, showing no fear. I felt highly honored, and a warm feeling came over me.

During those years that I lived in Alaska, Admiralty Island was a part of the Tongass National Forest and as such was managed by the U.S. Forest Service. This agency had grandiose plans to clear-cut the island. Every watershed was to be stripped of its protective cover of virgin timber. Inevitably, this would have resulted in massive erosion, destruction of fish and game habitat and the wintering grounds of scores of trumpeter swans. A rich, irreplaceable, unique wilderness would be turned into a wet desert. The government people brainwashed the public with pious mouthings about "broad tax base," "multiple use," "development of resource" and "economic progress." What these people did not say was that Admiralty Island and its tremendous resources of fish and game was to be sacrificed to feed a Japanese-owned pulp mill located at nearby Sitka. Here every foot of timber taken from ravished Admiralty would be processed and exported to Japan to manufacture such glamorous articles as paper napkins and disposable diapers—trappings of an exciting and heroic civilization.

For reasons known only to God and the bureaucratic mind, the Forest Service adamantly denied that trumpeter swans existed on Admiralty Island. Such a statement was incomprehensible to any person acquainted with the facts. Down through the centuries, the resident Indians have known that these waterfowl wintered here. I visited at the head of a long tidal inlet, one day in January, which an Indian friend told me about. On that day, I counted sixty-eight trumpeters in an area not much larger than a football field. Frank Dufresne, Corey Ford and I saw several of these swans one summer while fishing for trout on the west coast of Admiralty, although we weren't looking for them. Bush pilots who flew over the island reported seeing them "all the time." Allen Hasselborg, who spent a lifetime roaming every part of the Admiralty Island, told me that he had seen "many, many" trumpeters in his life. It's significant that there is a Swan Cove, a Swan Island and a Swan Creek on Admiralty.

Fortunately, since I left Alaska, this entire area has been set aside as a national monument. Hopefully, generations yet unborn may see these noble birds in their wilderness habitat and be the better for it.

The summer I spent with the swans passed all too swiftly. The final week in July came. The days were noticeably shorter and the nights were becoming chilly. One morning I awoke to find the sky in the east blood-red—a sure indication that a spell of rainy weather was imminent. I broiled a young grouse over my last campfire, shouldered my pack containing all my meager possessions, and made a final visit to the swans. Then I started toward tidewater and the salmon creeks. I arrived there the same evening and was pleased to find great numbers of fish on the spawning beds and much fresh grizzly sign. Before bedding down for the night I visited the small tributary and the miniature pool where I had discovered the fingerling Coho salmon. The little fish was still there. There were no mosquitoes around so I cut tiny pieces of flesh from a salmon the bears had carried from the creek and fed these to my little friend. It took my offerings eagerly and I was pleased to see its belly swell as it ingested the nourishing food.

Through most of the month of August I lived with the bears on a watershed about twenty-five square miles in extent. I came to recognize nineteen grizzlies by sight and certain idiosyncrasies. For example, there was the sow with three cubs, another with two yearlings, still another wise old female with a single cub that she guarded zealously. There was a very large male that avoided, and was avoided by, all the other bears, a medium-sized bear with a prominent rubbed spot on its rump, and a potentially dangerous grizzly that limped when it walked and groaned as if in pain. With the possible exception of one or two animals, I believe that I knew every bear on that watershed.

Too soon the beautiful and memorable summer came to an end. I had to return to town to prepare for the fall hunts I had scheduled. But before leaving for civilization I returned to the tiny stream for one final visit with my piscatorial friend. Alas! The little coho was gone. I hope no kingfisher or prowling mink devoured it. I like to believe it left the pool of its own volition and entered the main river. Then, driven by instincts beyond the ken of man, it would go into the great Pacific Ocean and begin an odyssey that would take it down the coast of California and across the ocean to Japan, Siberia, and the Aleutian Islands. Finally, three years after it began life as an egg, it would return to the place of its birth to spawn and perish in this wilderness dying ground as had its ancestors since the Ice Age and before.

Back in town and faced with a pile of unanswered correspondence, bills, and a sarcastic note from the bank regarding an overdue mortgage payment, I yearned to be back with the swans, the bears, and the brave little coho. Now, these many years later, with my hair turned white, my muscles shrunk, and my eyes less sharp, I wish again that I could relive the Summer of the Trumpeter.

Living With the Bears

Very early in my career as an Alaskan bear guide I realized I didn't know very much about grizzly bears. I decided that if I wanted to excel in my chosen profession I would have to know more than my competitors about the behavior, habits, travel patterns, and idiosyncrasies of these animals, and to accomplish this I would have to do more than hunt them with a rifle. What I had to do was to live with the grizzlies in their wilderness habitat.

It wouldn't do merely to observe semi-tame bears in a park or sanctuary or from the safety of a tower or enclosed platform. It was necessary that I get down on the ground with the bears, adjust my behavior to theirs, eat what they ate, sleep where they slept, travel the same ancient trails they walked, and, if possible, think like a bear. This meant the elimination of practically everything associated with "camping out" in the woods, including conventional food. It was a big undertaking, and I wasn't sure I could handle it, but I had to try.

One evening late in June in the early 1950s I anchored my boat in a protected cove located in the northeastern part of Admiralty Island. I chose this spot because it was adjacent to a productive salmon creek that drained a thirty-five square mile watershed. This stream always had a good concentration of grizzly bears in the summer and as far as I knew there was no other living soul within a radius of thirty miles. It was true wilderness bear habitat.

The following day I made everything secure aboard my vessel and with the skiff moved ashore. I had a light sleeping bag, my .375 H&H Magnum rifle, ammunition, sheath knife with hone, a trapping hatchet, plenty of matches in waterproof containers, an extra pair of heavy woolen socks, a cast iron cooking pot with lid, and the clothes I wore. At the last moment I added a five-piece spinning rod, a reel, and a few lures. I had considered fashioning a spear from native materials but decided it didn't matter how I took my fish as long as they weren't bought in a store. Also, catching salmon and trout with a light rod is fun, and there is nothing inherently wrong about pursuing such bucolic pleasures as may present themselves in the course of living one's life. Even the bears do that.

I moved my meager outfit up the creek above a waterfall that was the limit of the salmon migration. There I spread my bag in the shelter of an ancient spruce, stuck my hatchet in a tree and hung the cook pot on a limb. This was to be my base camp for nearly two months.

Wild berries were just beginning to ripen and the first week I had to scrounge to get all I wanted. As the season progressed there was an unbelievable profusion of half a dozen varieties from tide water to the alpine meadows. The grizzlies favored blueberries and wild currants and I preferred these varieties too. I quickly learned to gather and eat wild berries the way the bears do, by stripping the bushes of berries, stems, hulls, leaves and eating the whole. If you're going to subsist on berries you had best be not dainty or you might find yourself suffering from malnutrition in the midst of plenty.

Catching salmon and trout was no problem. It wasn't even a chore—it was fun. I usually fished in the deep pool at the base of the falls so as to not disturb the bears that did their fishing farther downstream. I used barbless hooks so that I could release unharmed any salmon I didn't want. The salmon in the creek were small and one a day was all I needed for myself and to feed various visitors I had which I shall elaborate on later. Some of the fish I boiled in my cook pot; others I rolled up in the broad leaves of skunk cabbage and broiled in the coals of my camp fire. On occasion I would get fancy and stuff a salmon with blueberries before broiling. I ate the livers and tongues of the fish too. Those who are repelled at the thought of eating such things possibly never tried them.

One morning as I was dining on cold boiled salmon left over from the previous evening, I had a visitor—a blue jay. At times these birds are impudent and obstreperous but this one alighted on the limb of an elderberry bush and quietly stared at me as solemn as a young owl. Probably it had never before seen a man and was curious as to what manner of creature I was. When I finished my meal I placed a few scraps on a cabbage leaf which I carefully laid on the ground near where the bird was perched. For several minutes the jay alternated its attention between me and the proferred food. Finally it dropped to the ground and began pecking tentatively at the salmon tidbits. When it ate all it cared to, the bird daintily wiped its bill on the moss, shook itself vigorously and flew away into the forest. I hoped this well-mannered bird would visit me again, but it never returned. Perhaps it didn't like cold boiled salmon.

I had other uninvited but welcome visitors that summer. It would be nice to say they came to visit me but I'm sure it was the salmon I kept at my camp that attracted these charming creatures. Weasels were frequent guests. When one appeared I would scatter bits of salmon in my woodpile. So rapid were the movements of these tiny predators that when one dived under a log it would reappear so fast on the other side that I couldn't be certain there weren't two animals instead of one. I marveled that these diminutive beasts that weighed a few ounces lived in complete amity with the great coastal grizzly bears that might weigh fifteen hundred pounds. I suppose there is a moral to be learned from this observation but I don't know what it is.

Ravens, those wisest of all fowl, perched in the tall trees that ringed my camp and watched my actions. They were most wary and suspicious, seldom coming closer than two hundred feet. Even at that distance if I moved about they would fly away. However, as I could tell from the sign they left, these birds came into my camp when I was absent and inspected it in detail. On occasion I would hide scraps of salmon under leaves or pieces of bark. Invariably ravens would find and eat the bait. Once a marten came out of the surrounding forest and ran past me like a wraith until it disappeared into the woods again. This was one of only half a dozen of these animals that I have seen in all of the thousands of days I've roamed the wilderness.

Once a week I hiked to the beach to check my cruiser and to pump the bilge. At these times I would dig clams which I would steam or eat raw. I also gathered mussels, kelp and various other varieties of seafood that my old seal-hunting partner Sockless George had taught me to eat. As George used to say, when the tide is out the table is set. How right he was! In those halcyon days the Territory of Alaska paid a bounty on hair seals, so one day when one came too close to shore to look at me, I shot it. I took the liver, which compares favorably with deer liver. Then I towed the carcass to the mouth of the salmon creek, where the bears made short work of it in a remarkably short time.

In general, that summer, I ate what the bears ate but not everything they did. For example, bears are partial to the roots of skunk cabbage and expend prodigious energy to dig them out of the swampy ground where the plants thrive. These roots look good but have a horrible taste. One has to be a bear to appreciate this ursine delicacy. I also drew the line at eating raw salmon. However, I did manufacture a limited quantity of what I termed salmon jerky. I simply cut the fish into thin strips, dipped them briefly into boiling salt water and hung them to dry in the sunshine. During rainy weather when the creeks flooded and I couldn't fish, this product was my basic diet. The weasels that visited my camp seemed to prefer it to fresh salmon.

One day, while exploring a small stream tributary to the main creek, I discovered an excavation under the root structure of an enormous spruce tree. Although it hadn't been occupied recently, it was obviously a bear den. I crawled in to investigate. It was spacious, snug, dry, and clean. When the weather was foul I sometimes slept there. It might have been embarrassing had the original tenant returned and found me there, but that never happened.

Whenever it suited me and the wind was favorable, I would gather up a good supply of tough, dry spruce limbs and hemlock bark from dead snags with which I would build a fire much larger than the small conflagrations I used to cook my fish. Then I would strip down and hang my clothing on limbs to air out and dry. It was delicious to stand close to the fire, twist and turn while absorbing the heat and luxuriating in the warmth. A fire is a wonderful friend to the wilderness dweller. It furnishes light, heat, and companionship, and asks nothing in return except that it be fed a few sticks and chunks of bark. Some nights I stayed awake until nearly dawn, tending my fire, watching the stars and listening to the music of the wind in the trees. Civilization seemed remote and unimportant.

I have frequently been asked if I didn't get lonely in the wilderness. Lonely? Lonely for what? Why would I have been lonely when I had a fire, a rifle, plenty to eat and interesting companions such as bears, eagles, ravens, deer, otters, martens, beavers, and weasels.

Oh, I know what loneliness is. Once I was on Madison Avenue in New York City. There were thousands of people hurrying and scurrying by me. I felt suffocated, frightened and very lonely. I was lonely the time they wheeled me into the operating room to perform open heart surgery and knew that there wasn't a person in Seattle who cared whether I lived or died that day.

Yes, I know what it is to be lonely. I have lived a fair part of my life in the woods, alone. I have been cold, wet, hungry, discouraged, weary and sore, but I have never been lonely. I doubt that I ever shall be.

Unemcumbered as I was with the trappings and gadgets that complicate matters for so many who go to the woods, I was able to move about freely whenever and wherever I chose. One morning when I came out of the bear's den where I had slept that night, I decided to hike up a nearby ridge I had never explored. I planned to be gone only a short while and didn't anticipate meeting any bears, so I left my rifle at the den. Up on the ridge I found a well-traveled game trail that led upward through an open, parklike forest where hardly any underbrush grew. It was so pleasant and inviting that I could not resist following the trail, though I found myself wishing I had brought my rifle.

Two hours later I broke out of the forest into a region of alpine meadows, stunted evergreens, blueberry brush, mountain flowers, snow-fed rivulets and ponds. The berries that grow in the high country are larger, juicier and sweeter than those at lower elevations. I ate my fill and then like a grizzly bear whose stomach is full I lay in the sunshine and fell asleep. When I awoke I sat a long while enjoying the panorama of unspoiled grandeur that reached as far as I could see. I felt exalted. The sense of freedom and joy was akin to a spiritual experience.

I stayed in the high country all that day and night. Deer were everywhere; I must have seen a hundred or more. Grouse and ptarmigan were plentiful and I saw several grizzlies on the slopes, including a female with three rollicking cubs following her. That night was cold, firewood was scarce, and I spent more time rustling wood than I did sleeping. When it became light enough to travel in the woods, I started down the trail toward the bear den, picked up my rifle and resumed the business of observing bear behavior. The day in the alpine country was one of the high points of the summer. Another unforgettable experience occurred a few days later.

I had known for a long while that grizzly bears are active at night, but I wondered how they were able to catch salmon from the creeks in the darkness, or if they did. I tried to imagine myself catching a salmon at night with my hands and was unable to do so. If I couldn't see a fish in the stream at night, how could a bear? Bears are notoriously myopic and are unable to identify a stationary object much farther than a hundred feet distant. Was it possible that they sensed the presence of the fish in some manner we don't understand? Did they feel for them with their paws? Perhaps their night vision was acute like a cat's. The only way to find out these things was to spend some time with the bears on the creeks at night.

One evening in August, conditions were just right. It was a few days prior to full moon, a light but steady breeze was drifting upstream, and though the sky was overcast it didn't smell like rain. I took a circuitous route to the beach, swung toward the tidal flats and began wading upstream to avoid leaving man scent that would spook the bears. By the time I had reached a log jam that I planned to use as a blind, I had filled my hat with wild currants to munch during the night. I laid my rifle on a gravel bar and squirmed my way into the maze of logs until I found a comfortable place to sit. Then I settled down to wait and watch.

In the daytime, an Admiralty Island salmon stream during the spawning season is a busy, noisy place. There are always bald eagles flying up and down the waterway or resting in tall trees, uttering their mouselike squeaking that sounds so ridiculous emanating from so fierce-visaged a bird. Bonaparte gulls wheel and pirouette over the spawning fish like a troupe of ballet performers. Back in the dark forest ravens talk to each other, to the bears and perhaps to things unseen and unknown to mortal man. Of course there are grizzly bears, too. Every creek on the island has its quota. One doesn't always see them, but they are there.

On this night none of the familiar sights and sounds were evident. Except for the sound of running water, the splashing of salmon and the querulous call of an unidentified bird far back in the gloom of the forest, the night was still. Everything appears different and distorted by the light of the moon. Inanimate objects and shadows take strange shapes and appear to move. I found myself gazing at a large dark spot at the edge of the creek about a hundred feet upstream. It was just about the right size to be a grizzly bear. The longer I stared the more I was convinced it *was* a bear. I imagined that I could see its legs, the ears and even its eyes. The creature was looking right at me! I closed my eyes to rest them. Then I looked up at the moon where it shone through the overcast and at the trees that bordered the creek. When finally I looked back at the dark object, it didn't resemble a bear at all. It was only a shadow. A bit later when I was unduly startled by the noise of a beaver slapping its tail on the surface of the water, I knew I was becoming jumpy. I glanced at my watch and estimated that dawn would break within an hour. The wind that came down the stream was chilling. Since I was learning nothing about bear behavior, I wished the night would end.

Far back in the woods there came again the petulant call of the bird I had heard earlier in the evening. I was wondering what species of bird it was that sang so mournfully when I happened to glance upstream. There, standing in the middle of the creek a short hundred yards away was a grizzly bear. Every man who has hunted bears very much is familiar with the phenomenon of these animals seemingly appearing out of nowhere. You may watch an area studiously and carefully for hours and see no sign of life, then suddenly there is a grizzly where seconds before there had been nothing. As the beast started striding down the creek in the inimitable manner of grizzlies—arrogantly, majestically, ominously, and as silently as a cat—I recognized the animal. I had seen that bear several times

174

during the summer. It was the largest bear on the watershed and walked with a pronounced limp due to some injury of the right foreleg. All objects look larger in the gloom of night, so that as the bear came closer it began to assume gargantuan proportions. It looked as large as a buffalo or an Angus bull. My heart began to pound and I could feel the skin tighten over my forehead. Involuntarily my body was preparing itself to fight or flee, but I had no intention of doing either.

Situated as I was behind the barrier of logs, I was as safe from attack as though in a steel cage. When the bear reached the logjam it stopped and remained motionless a full minute. It was so close I could see its nose crinkle as it tested the air. If I had been carrying my spinning rod I could have touched the beast, and the pungent, exciting odor of the grizzly was well nigh overpowering. Suddenly the bear dived into the stream and came up with a salmon in its mouth. It carried the flopping fish to a gravel bar and began devouring it. The sound of the bear's chomping resembled a man with good teeth eating a ripe apple. After eating the fish, the beast walked around the logs and came so close to my rifle lying on the gravel that I feared it might step on the weapon and break the stock or bend the barrel. Finally the huge bear, still moving as silently as a disembodied spirit, disappeared into the woods and I saw it no more that night.

The Eastern sky was beginning to lighten, when I heard a fearsome caterwauling up the creek as though a couple of grizzlies were engaged in mortal combat. I had heard these sounds many times before and knew a sow and her cubs were quarreling over a salmon she had caught. The notion that mama bear shares the fish she catches with her offspring is a charming bit of fantasy. Actually, the cubs are fortunate to salvage a few scraps after their mother has eaten what she wants. Out on the salmon creeks it's every bear for itself!

Through the years I have spent many nights with the bears on the creeks. They certainly catch salmon on the darkest of nights but exactly how they accomplish this I don't know. I am inclined

175

to believe that their close range vision is better than we think. During the several summers that I lived with the bears, I learned and practiced additional survival techniques. Salmon and trout as a steady diet became monotonous, so I rigged up a handline and, using salmon for bait, caught a variety of fish near shore in the kelp patches. These included such delectable varieties as sole, rockfish, snappers, and even halibut. One halibut I hooked must have weighed a hundred pounds. The fish was so big that I was afraid to take it into my skiff lest it demolish the frail craft in its struggles. So I towed it ashore and released it. I began carrying a .22-caliber with which to shoot grouse and ptarmigan. Spitted and broiled over a small fire, these birds are food for the gods. A few times, when it was inconvenient to build a fire, I skinned and ate a bird raw.

I never shot a deer during those summers because I would have been able to utilize only a fraction of the meat before it spoiled. Once, though, I shot a beaver from a pond near the headwaters of a salmon creek. Beaver meat is a gourmet's delight. In my opinion the wilderness offers nothing better, and this premise is shared by timber wolves and grizzly bears. I have known bears to dig a hole that would hide a truck to get into a beaver den. Wolves lie for days near a beaver dam, waiting for the opportunity to ambush one of these animals when it comes out of the pond to feed. When a wolf devours a beaver, it eats the fur, tail, intestines, bones, meat everything except the jaws and cutting teeth.

I dried the castor of the beaver I killed and carried it for years as a pocket piece. This gland exudes a tantalizing, fragrant, seductive odor that attracts any animal that I know of. Whenever I felt weary or stressed, I would hold the castor to my nose and inhale the fragrance. Invariably I felt better. Like many of the better things in life, it cost nothing and left no remorse.

After the first summer I lived with the bears I decided that a short-handled ax would do anything a hatchet would do but do it better. In a short time I could build a lean-to that served as an effective windbreak, reflected the heat from my campfires, and kept me and my sleeping bag dry. With an ax I could fall dead snags that furnished me with a bounteous supply of fuel, thus saving many hours of foraging for wood each day. I had three hundred old-fashioned kitchen matches, which I carried in two waterproof plastic bottles. With that supply I could have lived in the woods six months and still had matches to spare. From long experience I learned to start a fire in any weather, under any condition with only a match or two. There is always plenty of pitch and dry wood if you know where to look for it. No man should venture into real wilderness unless he knows how to build a fire.

My diet was unbalanced and irregular. Whenever I was hungry I ate what was available. If no food was available I waited until it was. Just like a bear. One summer a storm blew up from the southeast, and it lasted several days. The creek became muddy, the salmon wouldn't take a lure, and it was too rough to fish in the bay with my skiff. As a result I subsisted on wild berries. It was wet and cold out there in the brush foraging for blueberries. I was tempted to go aboard my boat, start a fire in the oil stove and cook a hot meal but I resisted the impulse. I'm glad I did. Even when things didn't go smoothly I was happy, healthy and I felt good. I want to stress that: *I felt good.*

In October, 1974, after undergoing open heart surgery, I left Alaska for what I thought was the last time. I went to southwestern Florida to recuperate and live out my days in that balmy climate where grizzly bears, salmon and blueberries cannot live. Recovery was slow and uncertain. For three consecutive years I had additional surgery. The last time the surgeons opened me up they discovered a malignant tumor. Cancer. Inoperable. Bad news, they said. My days were numbered.

Since my days were numbered, I decided I might as well live it up and enjoy what time I had left. I began taking long walks on the white sand beaches and swam in the warm waters of the gulf. I fished offshore for grouper and yellowtail and in the

Everglades for bass. I watched the sunsets and wondered how many more I would see before the final one. I wrote a book, which was published and got good reviews. Months passed and then years and I didn't die. I was so busy that I forgot my days were numbered. In 1981 I had a complete physical checkup. The examiner could find no indication of cancer. I sought a second opinion a few months later. Again—everything normal— no malignancy apparent.

I knew what I had to do. I would return to Alaska.

Return to Alaska

When I returned to Alaska after an absence of eight years in the summer of 1982, I expected to find some changes and I wasn't disappointed. The jet landed smoothly on a mile-long airstrip where forty-years before the timber wolves used to assemble on cold winter nights to howl their lament to the moon and stars. Close by the airport were dozens of tents laid out in a geometric pattern. "Tent city," someone said. "That's where the migrant workers live."

"Tent city," I muttered. "By golly, I used to hunt deer right there where those tents are."

"Well you won't hunt deer there anymore," replied my informant. "Nobody hunts deer around here anymore. They're so scarce they got a closed season on them."

Deer scarce? Closed season? How could that be? When I left Alaska, the game biologists told us there were too many deer and that the range was overbrowsed. To remedy the situation, the state lengthened the season and increased the bag limit. When the winter snows drove the deer from the mountains onto the beaches, practically everyone who had an aluminum skiff, an outboard motor, and a rifle went deer hunting. The

181

slaughter was on. They killed bucks, does, fawns—anything with four legs. It wasn't long until there was plenty of browse but no deer to utilize it. Now the deer season was closed. The game department was actually planting deer where only a few years ago they were abundant. Yes, I thought, Alaska had changed!

I remained in Petersburg only long enough to borrow a skiff and assemble a spartan outfit. I had a sleeping bag, a plastic tarp, some emergency rations, outboard fuel, and my .375 rifle. I cruised along the mainland shore in a northwesterly direction. Each evening I made camp in one of the bays, fiords, or inlets that are numerous along the Alaskan mainland. At first I found no change in these places I visited. The creeks had plenty of salmon and trout. I saw a few black bears, mountain goats, mink, and many geese, ducks, and eagles. One day on my odyssey I went to the head of a long twisting bay, up the river at the head and into a deep lake several miles long. At the head of the lake there lies a beautiful meadow, walled in by mighty peaks where there are snow fields and glaciers that existed before there were men or even sub-men on this earth. In the meadow I saw moose, wolf, and bear sign. Seals came close to my drifting boat and gazed at me out of their mournful, liquid eyes. At the edge of the meadow, blueberries grew in profusion and I ate my fill. Then I lay in the warm sun and slept. Once more I was in a true wilderness, miles from any other person. I felt good. I was happy. I envied no other person.

Not far from the meadow a clear, cold, spring-fed creek flows into the lake through a grove of big timber. Many years before Herman, a prospector I had known, had built a cabin here. It was a good cabin and even had a window. Not all cabins in remote wilderness areas have windows, you know. I had planned to spend the night in Herman's old home but when I went there, the only trace that remained was the rotted base logs of the cabin and a few moss covered stumps. The cabin was gone and its builder too, I supposed.

Herman had roamed the mountains and valleys of the southeastern Alaska mainland for half a century or more. He was my friend and I knew him well. Carrying a prospectors' hammer, rifle and magnifying glass, he labored mightily searching for gold, gold, always gold. And he found gold. He showed me his samples. Looking at these through his magnifying glass, I could see the minute yellow specks of the stuff. But there was never enough. At times Herman had to trap mink and marten awhile to get another grubstake. I wonder whatever happened to Herman. Probably he died out there in the wilderness, and his body returned to the earth from whence it had sprung, as his cabin had done.

I would have enjoyed staying awhile at this delightful place, but the Alaskan summers are short and there was much I wanted to do. Reluctantly, I left the serenity and beauty of the lake and meadow to the denizens of the wilderness and continued my journey northward.

A few hours later I came into an inlet that I remembered as being singularly beautiful. One winter I took eighty-four pieces of fur there in three weeks. I might have doubled my catch but I wanted to make certain I left plenty of breeding stock. It will be many years before anyone takes any fur from that area again. The loggers had moved in. Another piece of our vanishing wilderness was being turned into a sullen, ugly, eroded wasteland. No regard was being given to wildlife resources or the preservation of watershed and recreational values as required by congressional law on national forest land. I found two black bears that had been shot and left to rot. Although there wasn't another inhabitant for twenty miles, not one of those loggers professed to have any knowledge of who killed those bears. One jokester suggested that they might have died from "natural causes." He punctuated this remark with raucous laughter.

The same day I crossed Stephens Passage, which separates the mainland from Admiralty Island. When I pulled my skiff onto a gravelly beach and stepped ashore, I understood why travelers sometimes kiss the soil when returning after a long

absence from the land they love. I felt that way now. Admiralty—
Hootz-Na-Hoo, Fortress of the Grizzly, now a national monument. One million acres of pristine wilderness sed aside for the
use and enjoyment of all the people. Sixty-seven salmon streams
that would produce fish in perpetuity and would never be
dammed, eroded, poisoned, polluted or tamed. A million acres
where there would never be a road, neon sign, saloon, billboard,
garbage dump, or smokestack. An entire island where man
would not attempt to improve on the handiwork of the Creator!

When I moved my few belongings from the skiff to the timber
bordering the beach, I saw fresh tracks of deer, mink, and grizzly
bears. I spread my bag under a spruce tree near a bear trail, hung
my cooking pot on a limb and lay on the soft warm moss to rest
awhile. It was so comfortable and peaceful that I fell asleep.

When I awoke, I hiked through the woods to a nearby creek
where I used to bring clients to hunt bears. The salmon run was
just starting, so there were few fish in the stream. Hiking
upstream, I crossed a meadow where I spotted a doe with two
fawns. They weren't unduly alarmed. Placing their feet daintily
and walking stiff-legged, they moved ahead of me and disappeared into the forest. I spent most of the afternoon prowling
along the creek. Though I saw no bears, one snorted close by in
the brush. That evening I ate two handsome, pink-meated Dolly
Varden trout that I'd broiled over my campfire. That night I
slept snug and warm in my bag twenty feet from a well-traveled
bear trail. When I wakened the sun was high in the sky. I had
slept nine hours. In town I rarely sleep longer than five.

The weather was remarkably pleasant. Day after day it was
warm, sunny, and calm. I walked the bear trails, across endless
muskegs, through solemn, brooding rain forests and hiked up a
dozen salmon creeks where the grizzlies were beginning to
congregate without ever seeing another human being. There
were bears on all the creeks but not as many as there were a
decade ago. And the bears, on the average, were definitely
smaller. All summer I did not see the track of a really large bear.

Perhaps regulations should be changed to reduce hunting pressure. With wise management the Admiralty bears will do more than just survive; they will thrive and grow to maximum size as they have in past years.

One of the streams I visited drains a short watershed, walled in on three sides by mountains of spectacular beauty. A score of waterfalls cascade down sheer cliffs from the glaciers and snow-fields above. Barely two miles long, this stream is one of the most productive salmon creeks in southeastern Alaska. In the fall bears come here to feed in great numbers. The two largest grizzlies that my hunters took during the thirty years I guided were both killed on this watershed in successive years within a few hundred feet of each other.

In any one of the continguous United States this resplendent valley would be famous as a tourist attraction. People would travel great distances to fish the waters and enjoy the pristine grandeur. In all Alaska a mere handful of people were even aware of the existence of this unnamed valley and stream.

During my career I often brought clients here to hunt bears or to fish. We had good success hunting bears but mostly I remember the valley for the unbelievably superb trout fishing. As I hiked along the bear trail that follows the contour of the creek, carrying only a spinning rod and my rifle, I wondered if anything had changed since I had been there a decade before. An hour later I came over a low brushy hill and dropped down to a still stretch of the river about the length of two football fields, twelve-feet-deep and a stone's throw wide.

Long before I was born an ambitious colony of beavers had dammed the stream here, creating a miniature lake. With the passage of time the furred engineers had eaten the food and moved to greener pastures. The dam fell into disrepair and finally disappeared, but the impoundment they had created remained. It became a nearly perfect place for migrating salmon and trout to rest before ascending further upstream to spawn.

Nothing had changed since I had been there years before. Certainly no one had fished here that year or perhaps for many years. So many trout were in the pool that I couldn't see the bottom. They weighed from one to four pounds each, and there were thousands of them. I remembered the time I brought two sportsmen from Tennessee to this spot. One of them, using a light spinning rod and a variety of lures, caught and released trout until his arms became weary. Then he sat on a log to rest. "I can't believe it," he kept saying, "I just can't believe it." At last he cleaned out his tackle box, seeking a lure the trout would *not* strike. He could not find one. That evening in camp this gentleman told me that he had fished every major trout stream in the United States. Not one of them, he said, compared with this nameless creek he had fished that day on Admiralty Island.

The day I spent alone on that unnamed, rarely visited creek was a high point of my 1982 summer excursion. Resting on the mossy ground, my back against a tall spruce, I gazed utterly fascinated by the idyllic beauty all about me—the waterfalls cascading down the cliffs, the clear creek, the wildlife, the virgin forest, the snowy peaks. Everything was in harmony, and nature was in balance, as it had been since the Ice Age. I was so engrossed in my thoughts that I reached the beach before it occurred to me that I hadn't caught a couple of trout for my supper. It took an hour to catch a few small rock bass near the kelp patches. These fish are fine eating but compared to trout not very glamorous.

Every renowned big game guide in North America has a favorite place to hunt. It may be a mountain, a remote watershed, an estuary or a valley that less experienced guides haven't discovered. When game is scarce, hard to find, or when time is running short, a guide can often take his clients to one of these places, find game and send his hunters home happy. Unless he can do this consistently, a professional guide may not stay in business very long. When I was actively guiding bear hunters I had several favorite places, but one in particular I favored above the others. It was a tidal meadow on Admiralty Island I described earlier in this book. Now that I was back in the vicinity, I could hardly wait to revisit the place that I had wondered for eight long years whether I would ever see again.

One evening when I spread my bag under a tree to sleep, a light rain began falling. A spell of sour weather seemed imminent, but when I awoke in the morning, the sun shone brightly in a flawless blue sky. A seal swam into the little cove where I was camped and raised its body high out of the water to inspect my skiff. In the outer bay I heard a whale blow, and a bald eagle stared at me from his perch in a nearby tree. All these things seemed to be propitious omens. And if that weren't enough I had dreamed that night that I was in the woods following a great blond bear that had turned and smiled at me! The tide was flooding; the weather was perfect. This was the day to visit my favorite place.

An hour later I beached my skiff and tied it to the same tree I had used many times in past. Then I hiked to a nearby promontory that was covered by tall grass to wait until the tide receded. What was now a shallow lake would then become a tidal meadow. Before I settled down to wait, I searched for signs that would indicate anyone had been there recently. There were no lunch wrappers, cigarette butts, match cases, empty cans, or any of the litter that man leaves wherever he goes. Certainly no one had hunted there that season. Perhaps many seasons.

Sitting there in the warm sun looking at the scene, I had a powerful feeling of nostalgia. It seemed only a short time before when I'd sat at this very spot with a genuine baron. That evening this pompous duffer, soft, fat, lazy, over-dressed, overfed, and senescent, was lying alongside me, snoring gently while I watched the meadow for bears. The sun had just set behind a mountain and the long sub-arctic twilight had begun when a magnificent male grizzly with a perfect pelt came out of the woods in the northeast corner of the meadow. He stood for a

187

few moments, testing the wind and surveying the scene. I felt the hair on the back of my neck rise, as it always does, when I see a really large grizzly bear. Then the mighty beast started walking at a steady four-mile-an-hour pace toward the west. Undoubtedly he was aprowl in search of a mate and I knew exactly what the bear would do. He would follow the bear trail that followed the contour of the shoreline. Directly opposite our position was a rocky point about four hundred yards distant. The bear would reach that position in thirty minutes. All we had to do was walk less than a quarter of a mile over flat ground while the grizzly traveled two miles. It was a lead pipe cinch. There was no way we could fail to get that trophy bear.

Gently I shook the baron awake and showed him the bear. His eyes got large as saucers. His face reddened and his nostrils twitched like a rabbit's. I hoped he wouldn't faint. I explained the situation to him. "Strip down," I said. "Take off a few layers of clothes. I'll walk slow while you follow me over to that rocky point where we'll ambush the bear."

A strange look came onto the old gent's face. "No!" he said. "I refuse."

I was flabbergasted. I pleaded, I conjoled, I entreated. I even became mildly abusive. But the baron was adamant. He simply refused to walk a short distance over ground that a five-year-old child could have negotiated to take the trophy for which he had traveled many thousands of miles. "There will be other bears," he said. There were other bears on that trip but none like that one.

Back in the woods a piece I came onto the remains of a fire I had built at the base of a dead spruce. At the time I was guiding Jack O'Connor and Lew Bulgrin. It had been a raw, windy, wet day in May. The chill factor was wicked. What had started out as just another day of bear hunting was rapidly becoming a matter of survival. I had to take these men back to the boat where they could thaw out or build a fire. I decided to build the fire. While we were warming ourselves and drying our outer clothing, I stepped from the woods to look at the meadow. Close by, within easy rifle range, were four grizzly bears—a sow with three spaniel-size cubs. The bears were completely oblivious to our presence and stayed in the open for an hour before returning to the shelter of the forest. They never were in any danger from us—no decent sportsman would consider shooting a female bear with cubs. Both Jack and Lew have gone over the Great Divide, and I'm sure the bears have, too.

When I came to the salmon creek at the head of the meadow, memories of the past nearly overwhelmed me. Over here, Charley, a young man from San Angelo, Texas, had made a one-shot kill of a running grizzly with a .270-caliber rifle. Over there was the log I had been sitting on with a hunter from New York when a bear had suddenly jumped up on the same log we were on and began walking toward us. It could have been a touchy situation but before either of us could bring our rifles into position, the brute leaped off the log and went crashing through the forest, making as much racket as a tractor. Looking out over the open flat, I recalled the time a client and I had made a half-mile stalk on a fine trophy-size brownie. It took a long while, but finally we got so close to the unsuspecting animal that we dared go no farther lest the beast hear or see us. The bear was partly hidden by a patch of heavy brush. I told my hunter to hold his fire until the animal moved enough to give him an unobstructed shot at its shoulder. All that was required was for the bear to move four or five feet to the right. So we waited. And waited and waited. While we waited, the no-see-ems went to work on us. They crawled into our nostrils and ears. They sucked our blood. They swarmed about our faces so thickly that our vision was obscured. Carefully and surreptitiously, we brushed them from our naked skin but immediately a fresh contingent replaced those we had destroyed. All the while we endured the torture the bear continued to feed as placidly as a cow in a pasture. I was beginning to wonder how much longer I could endure the misery when the big bear made its move. The trouble was it moved in the wrong direction. It went back into the deep forest and we saw it no more. Bear hunting is like certain other sports—you win some and you lose some.

I wandered up the creek and through the woods all that day. I tried to remember how many bears my clients had taken in this two square mile area over a period of thirty years. The best I could do was to come up with an approximate number. I reluctantly left the place that evening when the tide was full. It was the only time I had been there that I hadn't seen at least one bear.

Admiralty Island is still a wilderness wonderland. Because of its status as a national monument, it will be safe from the despoilers and developers in the foreseeable future. No roads will be built, no exploitation, no fences, no airport, no Keep Out signs. Within the century this million-acre island may support the last significant concentration of wild grizzly bears on our planet.

On my return trip to town I cruised along the north shore of Kuprenof Island. On each of three successive nights I camped at various coves and estuaries where I used to hunt in the past. Each day I walked along miles of beach and roamed the woods and muskegs but saw nary a deer. Worse yet I didn't see even the track of a deer. I couldn't believe it. Only a few years ago when I used to hunt that area, deer were abundant. Now there were none. Perhaps it's a coincidence but it's a fact that the decline in the deer population of southeastern Alaska has been in direct ratio to the increase of clear cutting of the forests. The well-known maxim that the deer follow the ax may be true in Pennsylvania, Wisconsin and Alabama, but not in Alaska.

Alaska is my home. I shall live here until I die. And when I die I have willed that my ashes be scattered on Admiralty Island that I may be a part of the land I love so long as the grass shall grow and the sun shall rise. But I see and hear things that are happening on the Last Frontier that sadden and disturb me. Some of the most disturbing news involves hunters who illegally

190

kill game such as moose or caribou and leave the meat to rot. There is a different breed of people in Alaska now. A few years ago such action as shooting game animals for "amusement" was unheard of. Any person who did such a thing would have been considered a menace and handled very roughly.

The transition from a frontier to a more orderly society is slow and painful. Presently Alaska is undergoing such a process. There are problems. There will be greater problems. But there will never be any problems that Alaskans cannot and will not resolve. Certainly Alaskans will never allow their wildlife heritage to be destroyed or seriously depleted. I'm sure of that. I'm as sure of that as I am that the skies are bluer, the water sweeter, the air purer, the bears larger, and the mountains more majestic than anywhere else on earth.

The days are growing shorter rapidly. Soon the sun will barely clear the horizon. Then there will be a few hours of twilight and many hours of darkness. The snow will lie deep on the ground and the lakes will be locked tight as a drum. The bitter *taku* winds will howl down from the arctic north, and the frost will creep into the ground four, five, and six-feet-deep. But the winter will pass, and summer will come. When it does, I'm going back once more to Admiralty Island and live with the bears.

I'm looking forward to it because it may be the last time.